Business Engineering

Edited by H. Österle, R. Winter, W. Brenner

Rüdiger Zarnekow · Walter Brenner
Uwe Pilgram

Integrated Information Management

Applying Successful Industrial Concepts in IT

Translated by Therese Faessler

With 84 Figures

Dr. Rüdiger Zarnekow
Professor Dr. Walter Brenner
University of St. Gallen
Institute of Information Management
Müller-Friedberg-Straße 8
9000 St. Gallen
Switzerland
ruediger.zarnekow@unisg.ch
walter.brenner@unisg.ch

Uwe Pilgram
T-Systems CDS
Oberkassler Straße 2
53227 Bonn
Germany
uwe.pilgram@t-systems.com

ISSN 1616-0002
ISBN-10 3-540-32306-6 Springer Berlin Heidelberg New York
ISBN-13 978-3-540-32306-8 Springer Berlin Heidelberg New York

This work is subject to copyright. All rights are reserved, whether the whole or part of the material is concerned, specifically the rights of translation, reprinting, reuse of illustrations, recitation, broadcasting, reproduction on microfilm or in any other way, and storage in data banks. Duplication of this publication or parts thereof is permitted only under the provisions of the German Copyright Law of September 9, 1965, in its current version, and permission for use must always be obtained from Springer-Verlag. Violations are liable for prosecution under the German Copyright Law.

Springer is a part of Springer Science+Business Media

springeronline.com

© Springer Berlin · Heidelberg 2006
Printed in Germany

The use of general descriptive names, registered names, trademarks, etc. in this publication does not imply, even in the absence of a specific statement, that such names are exempt from the relevant protective laws and regulations and therefore free for general use.

Hardcover-Design: Erich Kirchner, Heidelberg

SPIN 11672470   42/3153-5 4 3 2 1 0 – Printed on acid-free paper

Preface

After years of apparent dormancy, once again companies are paying more attention to information management. IT departments and CIOs are confronted with a number of new challenges, which force them to reconsider past information management strategies and solutions. Recently cited as positive trends in IT are only those developments concerning stronger customer service and process orientation or pertaining to new forms of IT governance. Questions about the efficiency and effectiveness of company IT utilization are once again taking center stage. More and more IT departments are under pressure to perform with regard to quality, functionality, and transparency, especially when performance does not mirror customers' requirements. The intensity with which discussions are taking place about costs, outsourcing, or offshoring between IT and other business units epitomizes this pressure.

This text addresses the challenges to information management. Using the model for integrated information management, this book presents a framework for the management of IT services and a tangible organization of information management. In defining the model we were guided by two principles. What consequences are there for information management in changing to an output oriented perspective, which is defined as a customer perspective of IT products and services? And which successful management concepts and methods from other industries, for example from manufacturing or the service industry, can be transferred to information management? These two leading questions, in conjunction with many discussions with managers from IT departments and business units, contributed considerably in forming this model.

The model of integrated information management presents a framework. We are aware of the various open questions, which can only be answered through further work and specification. Thus this book describes not the end of a development, but forms rather the starting point for further research and further discussion on a broad spectrum of topics in theoretical and practical information management. With this in mind we look forward to diverse and prolific feedback. Many people have contributed to this book with their ideas and concepts. We thank the partner companies of the "Integrated Information Management" Competence Center, in particular Altana Pharma, Deutsche Bahn, Deutsche Bank, Deutsche Telekom, and the Swiss Federal Department of Justice and Police, all of whom were actively involved in the specification of the model since 2002. Additionally Axel Hochstein, Jaroslav Hulvej, and Jochen Scheeg made important research contributions. Their contributions are noted in the text.

St. Gallen, in January 2006   The Authors

Table of Contents

1 Introduction 1
   1.1 The Status Quo of Information Management 1
   1.2 The Role of IT Services in a Company 3
   1.3 The Production of IT Services 5
   1.4 Integrated Information Management 6
   1.5 How the Book Is Structured 8

2 Information Management: Developments and Challenges 9
   2.1 From IT Department to IT Service Provider 9
      2.1.1 Context 9
      2.1.2 IT Service Provider 9
      2.1.3 Core Concepts and Recommendations 15
   2.2 From a Project Oriented to a Product Oriented Perspective 16
      2.2.1 Context 16
      2.2.2 IT Services and IT Products 16
      2.2.3 Core Concepts and Recommendations 28
   2.3 Industrialization of IT Service Production 29
      2.3.1 Context 29
      2.3.2 IT Service Production 29
      2.3.3 Core Concepts and Recommendations 33
   2.4 Integrated Management of Portfolio, Development, and Production 34
      2.4.1 Context 34
      2.4.2 Integrated Management 34
      2.4.3 Core Concepts and Recommendations 38
   2.5 Life Cycle Oriented Information Management 39
      2.5.1 Context 39

2.5.2 Life Cycle Perspectives 39
2.5.3 Core Concepts and Recommendations 48
2.6 Standard Information Management Processes 49
2.6.1 Context 49
2.6.2 Reference Models 49
2.6.3 Core Concepts and Recommendations 60
2.7 Summary 60

3 Integrated Information Management 62
3.1 Model Overview: From Plan–Build–Run to Source–Make–Deliver 62
3.2 Model Components 67
3.2.1 Govern 67
3.2.2 Source 71
3.2.3 Deliver 80
3.2.4 Make 88

4 Practical Examples of Integrated Information Management 107
4.1 Six Sigma Analysis of IT Production Processes 107
4.1.1 Six Sigma Basics 107
4.1.2 Six Sigma Analysis of IT Application Support 110
4.2 Integrated Cost Accounting and IT Products 114
4.2.1 Status Quo in IT Cost Accounting 115
4.2.2 Integrated Cost Tables as Calculation Instruments 119
4.2.3 Prototyping Selected Elements 124
4.3 IT Applications Life Cycle Costs 128
4.3.1 The IT Application Life Cycle 129
4.3.2 Life Cycle Cost Analysis 130
4.3.3 Consequences for Information Management 134
4.4 IT Product Value Analysis 135
4.4.1 Principles and Fundamental Concepts of Value Analysis 136
4.4.2 Value Analysis for the IT Product "Email Service" 140

	4.5	Potential and Limits of ITIL Within IIM	145
		4.5.1 The ITIL Modules and the Levels of Detail	146
		4.5.2 Incorporation of ITIL in the IIM Model	147
5	**Summary and Future Prospects**		**152**
6	**References**		**155**
7	**About the Authors**		**158**

1 Introduction

1.1 The Status Quo of Information Management

No comparable factors exist for company success in industry and services which are so frequently criticized and so poorly rated as those of IT. Almost anyone can relay countless stories of IT projects not being finished in time, applications not being available, or employees sitting frustrated in front of far too slow PCs. Rarely does IT recognize the extent to which business is affected by its glitches. In many companies the exchange of information and data is not well organized. Even with electronic mail systems, the transmission of documents outside the company is tedious and a common calendar is somewhat rare. There are customers who are disloyal to their IT suppliers because they do not want to do without an umlaut in their name. As if this all were not reason enough for being dissatisfied, the whole business area is much too expensive. Having been the case for many years, IT management has more or less grown accustomed to this.

Surely this viewpoint is a little generalized. However, the precise analyses, which we present in Chapter 2, show that in many companies the effectiveness of IT solutions is often not proven and their efficiency insufficiently known. It is of no coincidence that there is a great supply of benchmark numbers for IT services.

IT is not left with only criticism. Frequently management recognizes that it is not able to judge its IT services, and therefore spins off its IT departments. This creates independent IT companies, which are to prove on the open market that they can make competitive offers and work efficiently. However, at the latest when resources and capital for investments are necessary for the new business field, management realizes that IT does not belong to its core business. And customers who were acting as guinea pigs in proving IT efficiency are left to deal with the consequences. IT outsourcing is a sounder alternative. In this case a team of specialists is entrusted with IT tasks, rather than relying on one's own competences. Collaboration is regulated with far-reaching and detailed contracts, thereby creating a basis for evaluation and price.

These are only some exemplary problems and challenges which information management deals with presently.

Information management is responsible, as part of overall company management, for the recognition and realization of the potential of information and communication technology in business solutions. In practice, the terms information management and IT management are frequently used synonymously.

In order to get to the roots of the described problems, it is worthwhile to consider the essence of IT management and compare it with that of the company. Several remarkable differences present themselves:

- *The IT process models are relatively new* (e.g. ITIL, COBIT) and represent a documentation of "Best Practices." The great attention and broad acceptance of these models show that until recently IT has been implemented rather unsystematically.
- *There is no continuously integrated quality management for new IT services.* The cost of bad quality, based on the employment of IT resources having no company benefit, is unknown. Surveys show that users have to deal with errors in more than 30% of all their work. These errors, independent of their cause, result in expenditures for which there is no company benefit.
- *There is no widely accepted cost accounting for IT services*, which could serve as a basis for cost management. Until now IT managers have concentrated on the accounting of initial costs. The executive committee for distribution has information about the costs of its sales applications with regard to computer performance and disk memory. However, it hears little about IT costs for processing and storing customer orders.
- *IT managers focus their attention on maintenance* of applications addressing core processes. First and foremost they practice management of changes in IT services as optimization of costs and quality of current systems. IT management pays the utmost attention to the scarce resource of "application developers." Interestingly enough, development costs of IT services for core application systems constitute rarely more than 20% of an IT budget.
- *The economic efficiency of IT investments is frequently based upon only the development and start-up costs of new or maintained applications.* The same applies to the prioritization of IT resources. To be noted, however, is that the operating cost of applications is significantly higher than the costs of development and maintenance of application systems
- *Initially installed and developed infrastructure for the production of IT services is infrequently examined for efficient utilization.* Additionally it is not adapted to prevailing needs. Retiring application systems and reusing technical platforms is rare.

Recapitulating, it can be said that in practice priorities and methods of information management are frequently characterized by a strong focus on the development of new applications. This results in too little attention being given to the management of operating costs and operating quality. As a consequence costs are frequently higher and quality worse than expected and necessary for the business units.

What is the advantage of new Customer Relationship Management (CRM) software if sales employees must enter their reports in pedantic dialogues, with poor response times? The advantage of IT services within business processes can only be fully realized when planned functions can be implemented at the expected level of quality. Criticism of IT is the inevitable result of the fact that IT users form their opinions based upon the current support of their work.

What do IT managers have to do for their services to gain wide acceptance? This is the fundamental question addressed in this book. In the introduction we present some fundamental concepts and terminology with regard to the role of IT services in a company, the production of IT services, and the requirements of an integrated information management.

1.2 The Role of IT Services in a Company

There is no doubt that companies are in urgent need of IT services. IT services should provide the basis for efficient business processes and guarantee the quality of the results of these processes. It is not possible to manage and control great quantities of and highly complex data without IT services. We position and structure the range of IT services with the following definitions

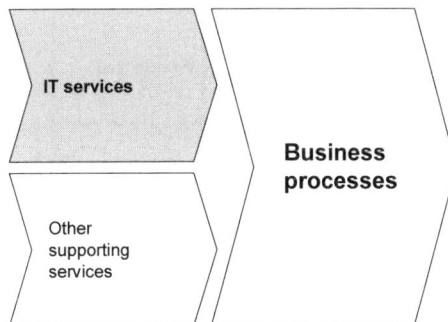

Fig. 1. The role of IT services in supporting business processes

IT services are services which support business processes in both industry and administration (see Fig. 1). IT services are produced through the operation of application systems. They are delivered to users of IT services. The benefit of IT services results from their utilization in business processes.

Information management has the task of producing IT products and services efficiently and in sufficient quality. Furthermore, according to changes in requirements of the business processes, to functionally and qualitatively modify and maintain these products and services.

4   Introduction

IT services can be classified in two dimensions; in their dependence on business processes and in their share of value creation in the supported processes (see Fig. 2). Listed by the link between service and business process we distinguish between:

- *Process neutral IT services*, such as email, calendar, text processing, business graphics, document management, etc. These services can be planned and produced without prior knowledge of the business processes in which they will be used.
- *Process related IT services for back office*, such as financial accounting, salary statements, controlling systems, cash management etc. These IT services are designed to support business processes, yet are only marginallly dependent on the business.
- *Process related IT services for middle and front office*, such as CRM, Enterprise Resource Planning (ERP), logistics (e.g. order handling, shipping), production systems, etc. These IT services are designed for support of the business process and are strongly dependent on the business.

Share in value creation

		Low share of value creation in process	High share of value creation in process	Product sold
Process orientation	Process neutral IT services	e.g. phone, fax	e.g. email, groupware	
	Process related IT services for back office	e.g. recruiting	e.g. accounting, controlling	
	Process related IT services for middle and front office	e.g. strategy development	e.g. CRM, ERP, logistics	e.g. electronic ticket, bank statement

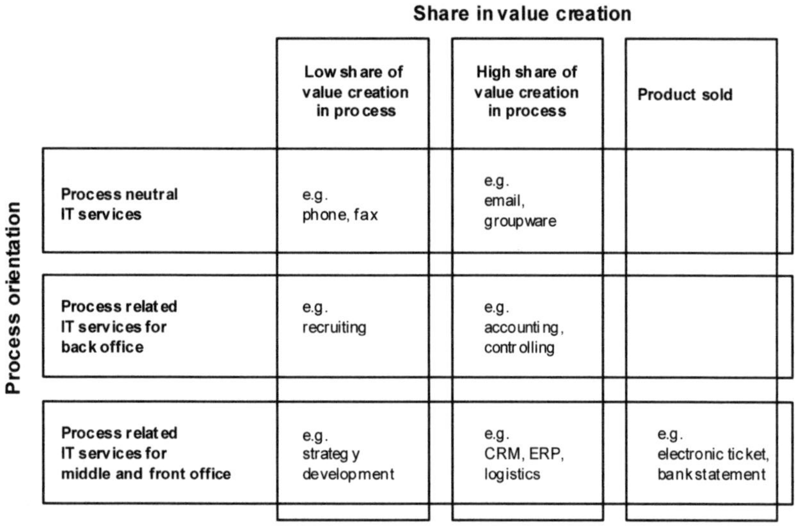

Fig. 2. Classification of IT services

Listed by degree of contribution to value creation we distinguish between:

- *IT services having a low share of value creation* in the process
- *IT services having a high share of value creation* in the process and substantial influence on the expense and quality of the process
- *IT services which are directly at the customer's disposal,* such as bank statements, electronic tickets, etc. This IT service production is exactly the same as the production process of the company.

This listing will support us in finding the appropriate structures for procedures in information management. The portfolio of IT services is structured so that its close relationship with business processes is emphasized.

The economic efficiency of IT services can be assessed by examining the relationship between the IT service effect on cost and quality of business processes, and the IT service production cost. Of course, these production costs include the application system's costs of production and maintenance and the costs of planning the IT services. This view of economic efficiency is necessary in order to make decisions regarding the provision of additional IT services. However, it can also be used as an element of control for examining the effects of IT services on business processes, in order to recognize the right time for terminating the provision of an IT service. This life cycle management of IT services contributes significantly to lowering IT costs.

1.3 The Production of IT Services

Before we discuss the management of IT services, we would like to briefly present the fundamental structure of IT service production.

Five production resources, presented in a very generalized and simplified way, are necessary to produce IT services:

- *Application programs*, in order to implement the demanded functionality of the IT service, the real "data processing," and manage the required data
- *Data memory* for storage and allocation necessary for the IT service
- *Servers* with operating systems and administrative software for the execution of all central algorithms necessary in the transformation of data and controlling the entire production process required for the IT service
- *Wide AREA network (WAN) and local AREA network (LAN)* for the data exchange between servers and users' workplace systems
- *Workplace systems* as instruments for entering and acquiring data, for information display and for the storage and processing of users' personal data

These five production resources can be thought of as "factories," which, cooperating closely, produce IT services. Each "factory" makes a specific contribution. A sufficient result is realized only when the contributions are correctly coordinated and configured. Application programs require special attention because they produce the demanded functionality of the IT service. Application programs implicitly steer the other four production resources. They more or less define, together with the quantities of IT services required, the total amount of investment required. They are thus a central cost driver.

Due to their close interdependencies to and on one another, optimizing production resources is a difficult task. To limit and optimize potential involves reacting to changes in one production resource and all of its triggered reactions on the other resources. This is a central task of information management planning. The method is to define and follow common strategies, collectively, for all five production resources, to specify and update technical standards and rules. In a field with rapidly developing technology this is a challenging, but worthwhile, task. Collectively composed and precisely formulated, as well as systematically defined and temporally maintained, standards work as an effective precondition for low costs and good quality.

For IT effectiveness to be achieved, it is important to be capable of changing the production resource "application programs." It is only with this capability that IT services can be produced, which meet new functional requirements of business processes efficiently. Projects play a large role in developing and modifying application programs. As previously noted, this is where information management usually puts the most emphasis and gives the greatest attention. However business process demands on quality and quantities must be realized as well. These demands are primarily on the other production resources.

Only when the coordination of all five production resources is guaranteed, is it possible to meet demands proficiently. Events, such as the temporal collision of an introduction of a new software version for processing orders, and software for an important selling campaign will become passé.

1.4 Integrated Information Management

The interdependencies of production resources presented above show that a vigorous integration of their management is necessary for IT services. Only with this management can an optimal realization of business process demands of functionality, quality, quantities, and costs be sustained. These demands are not unusual. Suppliers of services or products can only survive competitively when these customer demands are fulfilled constantly and consistently. It is obvious then that ideas should be sought in other business areas with demands similar to those in information management. The following aspects seem to be particularly important for a successful management of services:

- *The starting point of all activities is a comparison of customer requirements regarding functionality, quality, quantities, and costs* with current and future solution offers. This task is delegated to a portfolio or product management. The measures of success are customer satisfaction and the financial results of the products. The solutions are strictly defined products.

- *In designing the products all possibilities of production must be taken into consideration.*

- *Production is strategically aligned according to the requirements of product management* and vigorously supports product design.

- *Product development and production have independent strategies and goals.* The strategies and goals are closely coordinated and aligned according to customer demands.

- *Standardization and modularity, consistently implemented, make it possible to separate development from production.* Thus flexibility and efficiency can be realized simultaneously.

- *Production costs of the individual products are known.* There is a pre- and post-calculation as well as a product result statement. The extent of utilization of production resources is known and can, therefore, be optimized.

- *The production processes are documented and will be continuously updated through the quality and cost management systems of production management.* The same applies to processes for developing new products and improving production resources.

- *The procurement of production resources is positioned as a strategic success factor.*

Only a few substantial points are listed here. It is remarkable that such obvious information management tasks are perceived differently or not at all. This creates an accounting of the costs of resources instead of a cost calculation. Blanket Service Level Agreements (SLAs) are created, which only guarantee the quality of production resources (e.g. availability of servers or networks, etc.) and do not describe users' expectations with regard to quality (e.g. duration of a business transaction, email availability, or error handling time frames, etc.). What is actually required is a clear listing of IT services with guaranteed functionality, quality, and production costs.

In this book we want to describe an information management which focuses on the management of user product and service commitments. The goal of integrated information management is to identify, document, and meet these commitments with a continuous improvement of efficiency and quality.

Therefore this book addresses, above all, management, but also those who are searching for new ways to improve their IT services. We describe solution approaches and assist in the analysis and evaluation of your own situation. We do not attempt to present specific procedures or checklists or to give advice.

The statements made in this book are not to be interpreted as suggestions as to the organization of IT business units. We regard the production of IT services as a holistic process, which must be adapted to the individual company organizational structure. To that extent, this book is intended for all institutions which produce IT services, or plan and utilize them in their processes.

1.5 How the Book Is Structured

This book is divided into three chapters in addition to the introduction. In *Chapter 2*, we present six central developments and challenges which IT departments must consider. Based upon these developments and challenges, it is clear that today's concepts and methods of information management must be reconsidered and further developed in order to assure the effectiveness and efficiency of IT on a long-term basis.

In *Chapter 3*, our model of integrated information management is presented. The model divides information management into a framework consisting of four central components: Govern, Source, Make, and Deliver. Each component is described in detail based upon its tasks.

The fact that integrated information management is not only theoretical is presented in *Chapter 4* with the help of five selected examples. Each example describes a project which was implemented by the "Integrated Information Management" Competence Center together with a commercial working partner. The practical application of a component or fundamental concept of integrated information management was of utmost priority.

We strove to present the contents of this book to meet the requirements and needs of management from IT and other business units. We intentionally left out the underlying scientific theories and models of integrated information management, which originate from, for example, the business areas of industrial production, service management, and marketing. We would like to offer the reader instead feasible approaches to solutions and assistance.

> *In order to increase legibility, we highlighted central definitions, guiding principles, and recommendations in the text.*

Important approaches are supplemented with short examples from our experience.

2 Information Management: Developments and Challenges

2.1 From IT Department to IT Service Provider

2.1.1 Context

Today IT departments provide services within their own companies, in that the IT services support business processes and business products. IT departments are thereby developing into internal service providers. In the course of this development, the traditional roles and job allocations between IT and business units are changing. IT service providers must do more than the just handle IT projects and company IT infrastructures. We examine the effects of this development in the following chapter. The main focus is on the description of the interface between an IT service provider and its customer. This focus extends to the central role of Portfolio Management, which gains its importance in the design of this interface.

2.1.2 IT Service Provider

Presently, many companies are developing their internal IT departments into IT service providers. Frequently, through this development, organizational changes are carried out, for example, launching an IT subsidiary or service company. These spin-offs are usually provided with strategic objectives, i.e. the new company must be successful on the open market outside of its own company. In 2003 the magazine CIO published an investigation. The results showed that about half of all German DAX-30 companies spun off their internal IT units on the open market [Ellermann 2003]. However, in only six of the new IT subsidiaries was more than 30% of revenue generated from the open market. Thus the success of this strategy appears questionable. It is not surprising that counter movements are visible already. The trend is toward either re-integrating IT subsidiaries into the company or selling them off completely, in an effort to concentrate on core competences.

Independent of individual company strategy and organization, fundamental structures and relationships between IT service providers and their customers present recognizable patterns of interaction as seen in Fig. 3.

> The business units take on the role of customer and buy IT services in the form of IT products.

Business unit users employ IT services while executing business processes and thus produce benefits there. The business units have both internal and external IT service providers at their disposal as possible IT service suppliers.

> *Between customers and providers a market exists. The mission of this market is to align supply and demand as smoothly as possible. Whether the market is internal or external depends upon whether the customer is working with internal or external providers.*

The two market forms can be subject to different market mechanisms and regulations. Within an internal company market the regulatory framework design is a task of IT governance. For example, the way in which the formal relationships between customers and internal providers, tasks and responsibilities, legal and competition related questions, as well as service billing and accounting will be handled must be defined. When dealing on the external market, the legal and business frameworks are those valid for general business transactions.

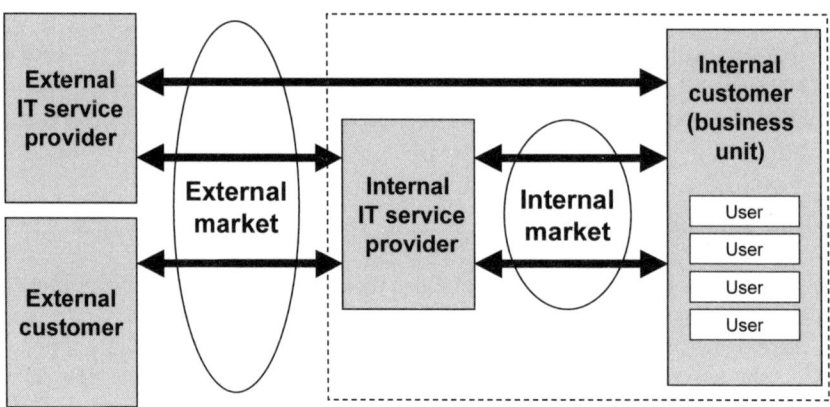

Fig. 3. Structures and relationships within a service oriented information management framework

For an internal provider different relationships can result from this framework. In addition to internal customers, An internal supplier can offer its services to external in addition to internal customers. Moreover, it is not compulsory that internal providers supply all services, but they can, for example in the context of an outsourcing agreement, act as a subcontractor.

The design of the interface between the IT service provider and its customer, the business units, is of utmost importance. The relationship and form of collaboration between the organizational units is altered. What was formerly an agreement between project partners becomes an agreement between customers and providers. The cooperation is modeled after open market purchase and sales mechanisms. It is not necessarily limited to dealings within the company. The IT service provider designs and produces IT services as efficiently as possible, in order to keep its competitive edge (see Fig. 4). The business units incorporate IT services into business processes, enabling an IT support of them. The advantage of IT services results in an increased quality and efficiency of the business processes.

The portfolio of IT services must be designed and controlled wholeheartedly by both sides. Thus, the Portfolio Management represents the central link between IT services and the other business units.

The business units specify the requirements of necessary IT services regarding quantities, functions, and qualities. They pay for required services. Using receivable income as a navigator, the IT service must define its priorities.

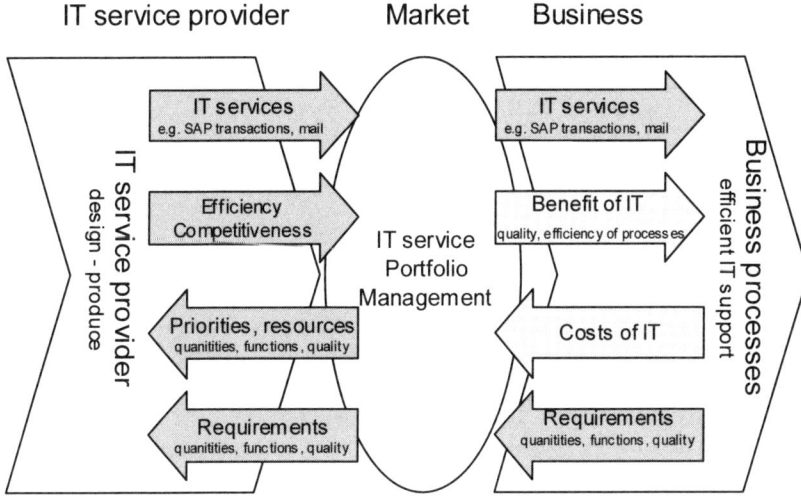

Fig. 4. IT service provider and business collaboration interface

Fig. 5 illustrates a process oriented view of the relationship between an IT service provider and a business unit. Both sides define a portfolio of IT services. The IT service provider presents all of the IT services it offers in the form of a portfolio of products. Based on its own requirements the business unit, designated here as customer, presents all of its required IT services in the form of a portfolio of demands. When the service provider makes an offer to fulfill a customer's demand, both negotiate the procurement conditions. The negotiation is concentrated specifically on the specifications of exact service characteristics (functionality), purchased quantities, delivery times, qualities, and the consequences of a breach of contract. The negotiation result is described and documented, for example, in an SLA. What is important to note here is that this agreement should describe customer oriented service levels (e.g. related to the business process, price, or customer satisfaction) and not technical service levels (e.g. availability ratios or response times). When an agreement does actually take place, this document is available immediately to both the service provider and service customer. The service customer can continuously monitor whether the service supplier is complying with the agreed efficiency factors.

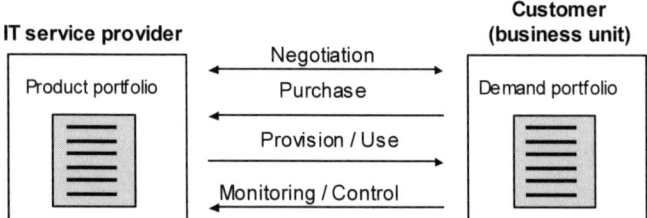

Fig. 5. Purchase and sales relationship between IT service provider and business unit

The real framework of the internal market between IT service providers and IT service customers is the subject of intensive discussions in many companies. For example, are internal customers allowed to buy IT services from external providers? Or is there an obligation to contract solely and exclusively with the internal provider? Can offers be sought from external providers in the sense of a benchmarking process? If so, how do these effect negotiations with the internal provider? Does the internal provider have the right to make the last offer (last call option)? Can internal providers offer their services on the open market? How are the potential resource conflicts between internal and external customers of an IT service provider resolved? And which market rules are the internal market transactions based upon? These are only some of the questions which need to be addressed in the context of IT governance.

The transition of a traditional IT department unit into a market oriented service provider does not always happen in one step. Rather, many companies pursue evolutionary strategies in which new individual participants and relationships are verified and accepted step by step. Example 1 describes such a strategy at a large Swiss company.

Ex. 1. From an internal IT department to an open market service provider

This example describes how a large Swiss company converted its internal IT department into an IT service provider selling services on the open market. The development took place gradually in the period 1989 to 2002.
Fig. 6 shows the four historical stages of development.

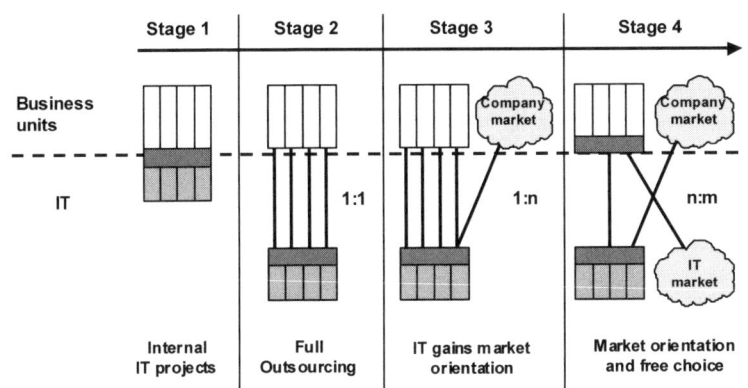

Fig. 6. Evolutionary developmental stages

Originally, the internal IT department realized IT projects for business units of the company (Stage 1). In a first step—for strategic, financial, and technological reasons—the internal IT department was fully outsourced to an IT service provider (Stage 2). A 1:1 relationship between customer (business units) and provider (IT service provider) was held firm. It was not possible to purchase and/or sell an IT service on the open market. In the next stage of development, this restriction for the IT service provider was waived. In an effort to open the market, IT services were made accessible on the external market (Stage 3). Finally, in the last stage, the restriction was also lifted for customers, i.e. business units now had the possibility of buying IT services from external IT service providers (Stage 4).

When tasks and roles are allocated between service providers and service customers, it is especially important to define who has or should have IT and/or business know-how.

The concept of IT and business know-how transfer between service providers and service customers must be designed, at best in accordance with the business processes being dealt with.

Fig. 7 illustrates three conceivable designs. Alternative A is characterized by an almost complete separation of know-how.

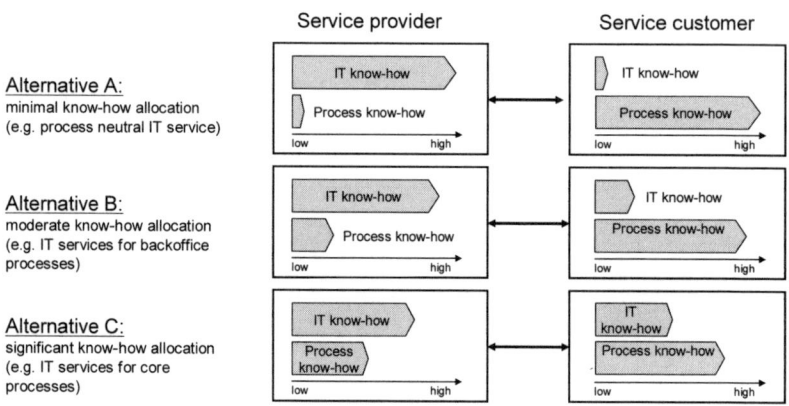

Fig. 7. Allocation of IT and process know-how

The service providers have exclusive know-how in IT. Service customers have exclusive know-how in business processes. This alternative can be advantageous with regard to business process neutral IT services, such as email, text processing, or document management. The service provider can assume all tasks of planning, development, and production of the IT service. Correspondingly, the service customer is responsible only for specifying the requirements on a purely business level. Service providers should not develop IT know-how in this alternative because their efforts would be unnecessarily engaged as resources, and thus would not be available for other jobs. It is therefore not efficient to develop service customers IT know-how in process neutral IT services, for example, over available software solutions for email services or hardware configurations of workplace systems.

The implementation of Alternative B is possible for IT services, where a certain level of IT know-how for the service customer and a certain level of business process know-how for the service provider are advantageous. Back office processes such as financial accounting or salary statements are appropriate examples here. The service customer should then "own" a group of IT specialists, who are primarily concerned with defining the requirements and project management with the service providers. Internal resources for development and production of IT services are available, if at all, only marginally. The service customer "owns" process specialists who concentrate on specifying business requirements, which form the interface to the service customer.

Alternative C is of advantage whenever IT support of a business process requires know-how to be widespread. In core business processes based on IT services (e.g. CRM or ERP processes) service customers have invested years in organizing complex IT solutions. Through this practice both IT know-how and resources have been developed. The results of these efforts are, for example, the existence of IT teams within customer organizational units. These IT teams actively collaborate with service providers in developing solutions or even assume development and tasks of production themselves. Through this collaboration the service provider has extensive business process know-how, which enables it to develop solutions independently and actively arrange cooperation with its customers.

2.1.3 Core Concepts and Recommendations

- The development of IT units into internal IT service providers will continue.
- The business units will take on the role of customer (IT service customers), IT departments the role of provider (IT service providers). Between customers and providers there exists either an internal or external market.
- The rules of the internal market will be defined within the context of IT governance.
- Portfolio Management is the link between the IT service providers and the business units.
- An IT service provider must continuously assess, plan, and direct the portfolio of offered IT services.
- The business units must develop a portfolio of requirements, in which the demand for IT services is identified.
- The allocation of business and IT know-how between service providers and service customers is unique for each business process and thus must be arranged individually.

2.2 From a Project Oriented to a Product Oriented Perspective

2.2.1 Context

An IT service provider sells IT services in the form of IT products to its customers. In this chapter we will analyze what exactly the products of an IT service provider are, and what the difference between an IT service and an IT product is. We consider what effect the product oriented cooperation between service providers and customers has on service providers.

2.2.2 IT Services and IT Products

Currently there are intense discussions in both theory and practice whether IT services are of strategic importance for a company, or instead only consumer commodities, like electricity, water, or telecommunication services, which can be bought and implemented as standardized packages [Carr 2003]. Although we perceive this debate as adding little to achieving any higher goals, it points to an interesting development. Business unit IT service customers are driven by the desire to reduce the, in their view, high complexity and obscurity of IT service provision. Instead of developing complex projects or designing application systems, of which there is only a minimal understanding of functionality, with IT service providers, customers wish to buy IT services in the form of pre-defined products. In our discussions with business unit representatives we were often confronted with the demand to be able to select required IT products from an IT service provider's product catalog. Of course this should be possible at a predefined unit price, in order to reduce high IT fixed costs and to be flexible enough to react to changing business requirements.

> *IT products form the basis of cooperation between IT service providers and business units.*

By definition a product is a good or service, which satisfies needs and can be utilized advantageously by the customer [Kotler 2002]. It is described by the dimensions of "type" (function range), "quality," "price," and "quantity." The product must be defined through a customer perspective. Accordingly this definition must be formulated such that customers understand it. The advantage of an IT product can only be realized in business unit customers' processes or business products. Usually the benefit of IT advantage cannot be realized with a single IT product, but instead by a bundle of IT products.

An IT service actually represents a bundle of IT services or products, which help in supporting customer business processes or business products and thereby create a business advantage (see Fig. 8).

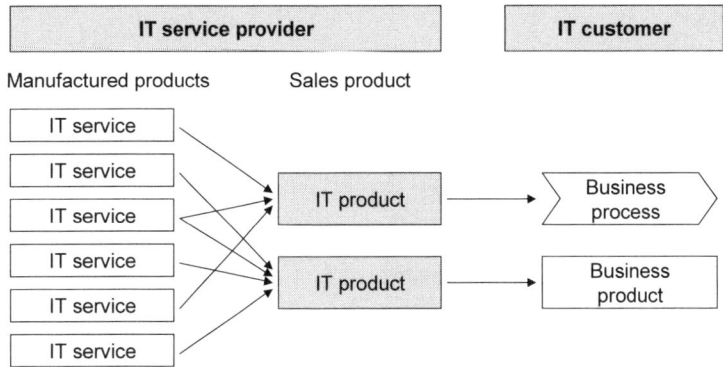

Fig. 8. IT services and IT products

To understand the IT product description, it is of utmost importance for the customer to understand the product's contribution to the business. An IT service is only then an IT product when it is represents an advantage while supporting business processes or business products. Similar to industrial manufacturing, IT services are comparable to manufactured units, while IT products are the IT service provider's selling units.

Fig. 9 demonstrates this concept of IT product visually using the example of a transportation company, whose business process "Produce Ticket" is supported by various IT services. The actual IT product includes all of the IT services employed within the business process "Create Ticket." Included here are, for example:

- *IT services in process step "Enter Ticket Data":* Preparation of a workplace system for salespeople; Development and maintenance of application system for data entry; Development and maintenance of application system for timetable information; Development and maintenance of timetable database; Supply and provision for computer and memory resources; Preparation for and provision of an IT solution for self-service terminals; Networking the decentralized workplace systems and self-service terminals; Support services (Help Desk) for collaborators.

- *IT services in process step "Calculate Ticket Price":* Development and maintenance of a central application system for transportation price calculation;

Preparation and provision of an IT computing center infrastructure for application systems; Networking of decentralized systems.

- *IT services in process step "Issue Ticket":* Preparation and provision of printers; Support and maintenance of ticket printers; Development and maintenance of an application system for the transmission of electronic tickets, for example, to cell phones.

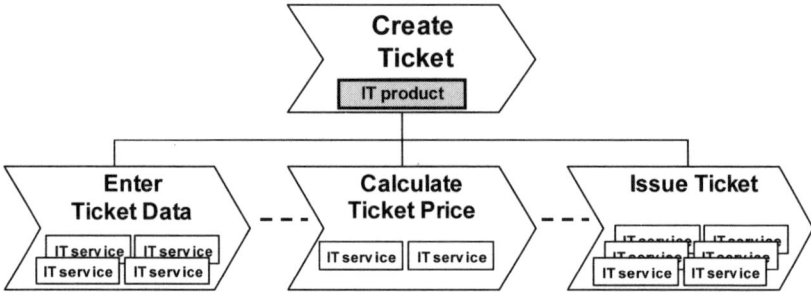

Fig. 9. An example of an IT product

No singular IT service is of use to customers. Only in combination do IT services benefit and support business processes and thus are considered an IT product.

The proportion of IT services within a business process can vary (see Fig. 10). In extreme cases a process can be made up of only IT services. Examples of such business processes are "electronic procurement" or "on-line banking" processes.

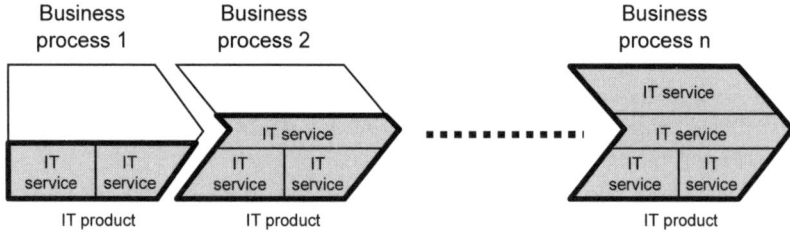

Fig. 10. IT products implemented as bundles of process supporting services

> *IT services can be standardized, in the sense of an unspecified customer mass production, or individual in the sense of a unique customization.*

Standardized services are primarily employed in business neutral or back office processes. Examples of this are invoicing, bookkeeping, purchase processes, or personnel processes. Individual customized IT services, in contrast, are found particularly in core processes of strategic or competitive importance. The individual customized design of IT services for processes such as those in CRM or Supply Chain Management (SCM) can create competitive advantages, which would not be attainable with standardized services.

What are typical examples of IT services and IT products in practice? An analytical evaluation reveals two separate categories of IT services and two of IT products (see Fig. 11).

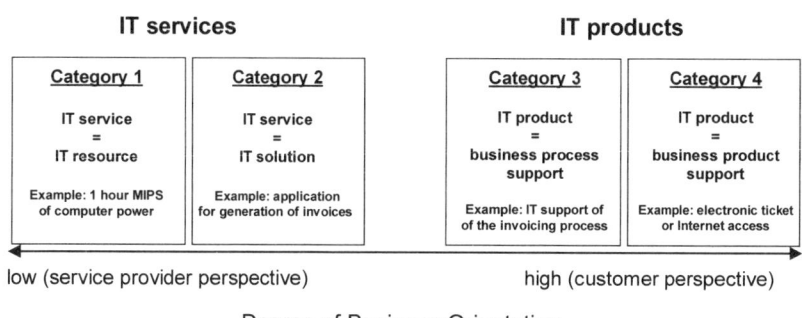

Fig. 11. Categories of IT services and IT products

Category 1 – "Resource oriented IT services"

Resource oriented IT services represent the past orientation of service providers. IT resources that are prepared and provided are considered services. Typical examples of resource oriented IT services and their corresponding unit sizes are:

- Provision of CPU time (1 hour of MIPS)
- Provision of disk space (1 GB per month)
- Provision of resources for EDP printing (1000 lines)
- Provision of resources for the development of software (1 man day)
- Preparation and provision of PC (month)
- Execution of technical transactions or jobs (1000 units)

The utilization of such IT services allows for a correct user allocation of IT resources. However, from a customer's point of view these services are actually inputs which only allow for a business oriented application when combined.

Resource oriented IT services are missing a business orientation.

If resource oriented IT services would serve as a basis for cooperation between service providers and customers, then customers would be forced to define contracts in technically defined units of which they have very little understanding. Customers would need to express their IT requirements as a combination of many individual services, which would necessarily increase the complexity and reduce the transparency of any agreement. Also it is extremely difficult for customers to estimate the required service capacities. For example, a customer can hardly judge whether the IT services necessary for the IT support of a business process (e.g. 80 GB per month disk space and 150 MIPS per hour of computer performance) represent the costs of an efficient, competitive measure.

Category 2 – "Solution oriented IT services"

Solution oriented IT services are a first step toward a stronger business orientation, by which the service provider is presenting an IT solution as its service. Application systems are at the core of such services, which is why solution oriented services are often found in software development. Examples of IT services in this category are:

- Preparation and provision of an IT solution for invoice processing
- Preparation and provision of a CAD solution for construction
- Preparation and provision of an IT solution for text processing
- Provision of a standard software solution for controlling

Solution oriented IT services represent, from a customer perspective, a first step toward a business oriented cooperation with service providers. Several IT services, for example, the initial development, which then goes into production and maintenance and the support of an IT solution, are bundled together by the service provider and negotiated as a sum total with the customer.

Despite these advantages the following still applies:

Solution oriented services are also not considered products because they do not offer customers business process benefits.

In analogy to industrial manufacturing, IT solutions can be compared with production plants, with which customers manufacture their real products. The production plant in and of itself is not useful to customers, but within it products are manufactured which support business processes and products. Thus, for example, from a customer perspective an IT solution for creating invoices presents no real business process advantage. Only a solution's output within the business processes, for example the completion of a calculation procedure or the actual entry of invoice data, has real business benefit.

Category 3 – "Business process supporting IT products"

Customers buy IT products to support their business processes.

> *The advantage and thus actual product of an IT service provider is a process supporting service. Process supporting IT products consist in practice of a multiplicity of individual IT services.*

Management and support services are also included in addition to the core services for the provision of hardware, software, and networks. Thus, in the previously mentioned example of the transport company, support services are provided in the form of Help Desks for supporting users, and management services are provided for the company's computer center.

Typical business process supporting IT products are:

- IT support of a personnel process (e.g. production of wage and salary statements)
- IT support of a procurement process
- IT support of an electronic selling process
- IT support of office communication processes (e.g. email service, text processing, Internet service)

In contrast to IT services described in Categories 1 and 2, service providers and customers dealing with process supporting IT products do not negotiate over technical parameters and functionalities, but instead over business oriented product properties and conditions. For example, in the previously discussed example of the IT product "Create Ticket," negotiations would concentrate on the following aspects:

- *Product properties* (to what extent is IT support within the business process necessary and what functionality must the IT product include)
- *Product quantity* (what is the expected number of tickets per month)
- *Product price* (per ticket)
- *Terms of delivery* (when and within which time period must the tickets be provided)
- *Product quality* (e.g. supply of a ticket guaranteed within 30 seconds with a probability of 99.9%)

The service provider makes the necessary production capacity available and produces the IT services required for the IT product. Production here means that every time a business process is executed, an IT product, in the sense of a process supporting service, is produced. For example, when a customer at a self-service terminal is provided with a ticket printout, at this moment an IT product "Ticket is Created" is produced by the service provider and utilized by the customer. Production and consumption of the product take place simultaneously, as is usually the case with service products.

Today, especially big IT service providers are already offering process supporting IT products for selected business processes. Example 2 presents such a product offered by the Deutsche Telekom AG.

Ex. 2. The Deutsche Telekom AG Central Billing Services (referred to as ZB) product catalog [Deutsche Telekom 2001].

The Central Billing Services (ZB) is the designated center for billing competence within Deutsche Telekom AG. ZB develops, operates, and maintains systems for the company subsidiary units T-Mobile, T-Com, T-Online, and T-Systems, which deal directly with external customers. ZB also supports the group service provider T-Networks Billing and Account Receivable solutions. T-Networks provides Deutsche Telekom AG customers with electronic billing and post-processing calculations. As one of the largest service providers in this market segment world-wide, ZB produced approximately 38 million bills monthly and provided 9.1 million individual connection reports in 2000. Altogether per month 6.1 billion service units required from 41 000 users were provided.

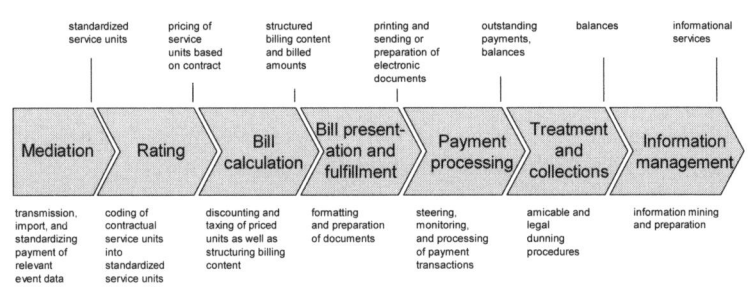

Fig. 12. Billing and accounts receivable process value chain

The ZB service portfolio is presented in a product catalog and covers Category 3 process supporting products. These are defined in addition to

> the value chain of the Billing and Accounts Receivable process, which is illustrated in Fig. 12.
>
> The service portfolio consists of products for each stage of the value creation process. Thus, for example, the product for the value creation stage "Rating" consists of the following standardized sub-functions:
>
> - Mapping of service units to contracts and products
> - Quantity determination
> - Allocation of prices
> - Accumulation of service units and production of object pricing
>
> The product offerings cover all required IT services necessary for the provision of the described value chain sub-function. The product price is negotiated on a Target Costing Basis and is based on the identification and measurement of the value drivers in the individual value chain segments.

The product prices, IT product functionality, and quality, which are negotiated between service providers and customers, have a crucial impact on the competitive capacity of the business products. The business significance is usually clearly higher than it is in the IT services and IT products of Categories 1–3.

IT Products and Outsourcing

In the current developmental trends in outsourcing, the shift in the concept of products from resource oriented IT services in Category 1 to business product supporting IT products of Category 4 is visible. This is demonstrated in Example 3.

The four categories of IT services and IT products are not mutually exclusive. On the contrary, they are often employed complementarily in practice. Service providers' IT products are made up of IT services (see Fig. 13). In order to be able to provide IT services, service providers must continue in working on IT projects, developing application systems, and operating and maintaining infrastructures. Therefore it is necessary for service providers to internally define their services on the basis of resources and solution oriented IT services. The business process and business product supporting IT products made for customers are the result of a combination and integration of the service provider's internal services. The internal IT services thus form the link between the service provider's IT oriented base objects (projects, applications, infrastructures) and the business oriented external IT products demanded by customers.

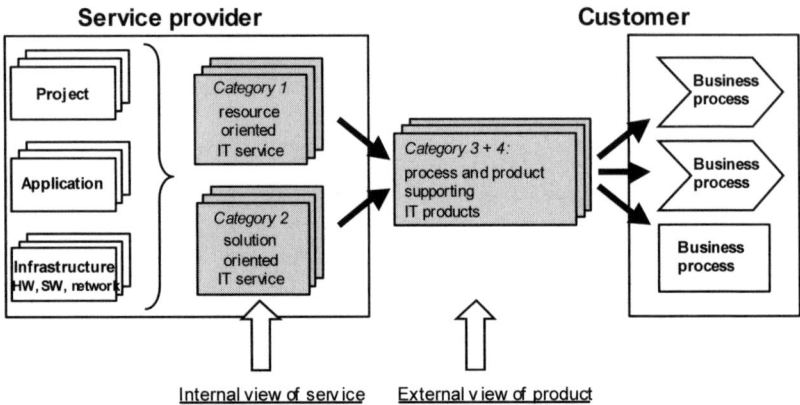

Fig. 13. Service provider's internal and external views of products

> **Ex. 3**. The development of understanding of IT services and IT products with regard to outsourcing.
>
> Outsourcing is a driver for the advancement of understanding IT products, since it is based on a clear separation of service providers and customers, as well as market oriented competition structures. The development of new outsourcing alternatives exemplifies all four categories of IT services and IT products described here.
>
> The basis for the classical outsourcing infrastructure is a resource oriented IT service understanding. Infrastructure outsourcing covers the migration of IT or parts of IT. IT resources are moved to external service providers. The service provider in many cases also assumes existing customer IT resources for which he must pay, such as assets or employees. Customers will receive a bill for the agreed price for the utilization of IT resources.
>
> Category 2 solution oriented IT services can be found at the core of new outsourcing alternatives, like *Application Management Outsourcing* or *Application Service Providing (ASP)*. In Application Management Outsourcing the service provider assumes not only the operation and maintenance of the application infrastructure but also the enhancements to the application. It is responsible for the application over its complete life cycle. Although the service provider is responsible for the application, it usually remains owned by the customer. ASP is a concept for renting application software, by which a service provider makes an application available and receives a rent, usually dependent upon use. The service provider owns applications and their required infrastructure.

> Business Process Outsourcing (BPO) is based on Category 3 process supporting IT products. In this BPO context, entire business processes or parts of them are moved to external service providers. Frequently the service provider takes on those customer resources linked to the business process, such as existing IT infrastructures, applications, and employees. The service cost accounting can take place on the basis of unit prices. Variable price models, which take into account different quantities of IT products actually used by customers, lead to service providers assuming a part of the customer's business risk. For example, if the process of bill creation is outsourced and the customer pays per bill created, then customer business losses, which lead to a lessening of bills created, directly affects the service provider's income.
>
> The migration of Category 4 business product supporting IT products leads to *Business Product Outsourcing*. For example, if a telecommunications company moves the IT services necessary for its business product "new telephone connection" to an external service provider, then it is considered Business Product Outsourcing. Similar to BPO, the service provider assumes a part of the business risk should variable price models be used. Should the customer sell fewer new telephone connections, the income of the service provider would be reduced.

Today, the requirements for a product oriented cooperation are being fulfilled in many companies. IT service providers are creating distribution and marketing organizations, designing product catalogs, or setting up service level managements. In the business units, departments have been designated to purchase IT products and proposals for purchasing strategies for various product categories have been designed: even approaches to redefining the role of the CIO to a Chief Sourcing Officer have been discussed.

In any case, the real implementation requires the creation of new roles and the rearrangement of tasks within the information management unit (see Fig. 14).

> *Product management is of utmost importance because it is responsible for both the service provider's sales of IT products and the customer's purchases of IT products.*

The chief responsibility of the customer's product management is to negotiate and buy the necessary IT products offered by the service provider. The respective business process managers can assume the role of the product manager for example. This makes inherent sense because these managers are ultimately responsible for the business processes and thus for the IT products needed during the business process. Alternatively, especially in larger companies, a central organizational unit can take on the role of product management (e.g. a CIO organization of a business unit).

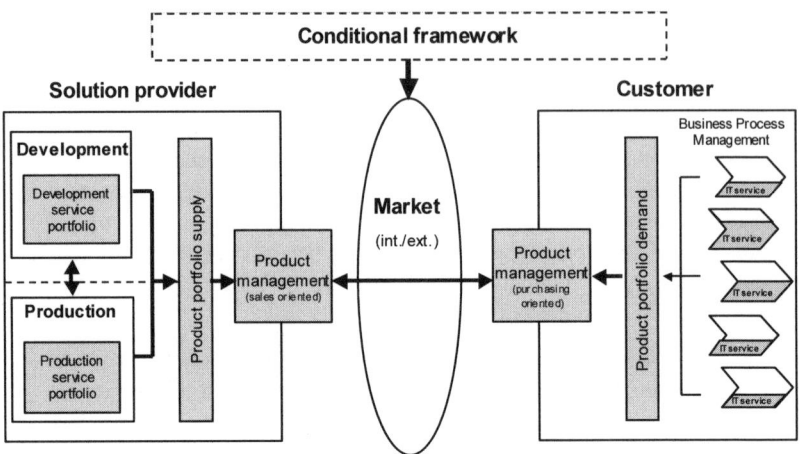

Fig. 14. The elements and roles of a product oriented information management

In the service provider's area there also exists a product management, which acts as an interface to the customer. The classical tasks of the product management are managed here, e.g. product development, introduction of new products, product support, market observation, and product controlling [Matys 2002].

The definition of the portfolio offering is a strategic task of management.

Usually a service provider has for both development and production departments independent service portfolios, which are made up of different services. Common development services are, for example, the supply of development resources or the development of application systems. In production, mainly operating resources, infrastructure components, or support services are offered. A central task of the service provider's product management is to combine the individual development and production portfolios to create an integrated portfolio offering. Customer oriented IT products can only be developed with this integrated approach.

The creation of the service provider's offering portfolio calls for an intensive cooperation between the development and production departments. Each IT product offered in the portfolio must be designed (i.e. developed) and produced (i.e. manufactured).

In order to create a portfolio offering which meets demand, an intensive interaction between the product management of the service provider and that of the customer is necessary.

	Traditional IT management	Product Oriented IT management
IT self-conception	Project developer and operator	Service producer
Basis for collaboration between IT and business units	Common project development	Product distribution and purchasing
Formal framework for collaboration	Contractual relationship	Market mechanisms
Controlling instruments	Project management	Product management
Internal accounting	Cost accounting	Product price
IT perception	Technical IT focus	Customer focus
IT behavior	Reactionary	Proactive
Reference object	Application systems; solutions	Products
IT base model	Phase oriented system view (planning, development, operation)	Integrated product view (product design and creation)
Business unit tasks	System requirement specifications	Product attribute negotiation

Fig. 15. Differences between traditional and product oriented information management

The effects of a product oriented information management become transparent when the differences between traditional and project oriented perspectives are specified (see Fig. 15):

- The self-conception of the IT department changes from one of a pure project developer and operator to that of a producer of products.

- The basis of collaboration between IT and business units is no longer joint IT project development, but the selling and purchasing of products.

- A consequence of the first two points is that the formal relationship between IT and business units is no longer characterized by a contractual relationship, but instead by competition oriented market mechanisms.

- The classical project management as a control instrument is replaced by the product managements of both the IT and business units.

- Service cost accounting is no longer calculated by means of a fixed cost key, but instead by the product price. This guarantees a user-fair allocation, because the user of an IT product pays directly by purchasing it. In determining a pricing structure, the service provider must calculate actual product costs.

- This new kind of cooperation leads to an IT department changing both its perspectives and behaviors. Technological characteristics are no longer the center of attention, but instead customer requirements. Instead of reacting to a business unit requirement by initiating a joint IT project, through a new customer orientation a proactive stance is taken by way of producing a portfolio of products. These will very likely be sold, thereby satisfying customers' demands.

- The fundamental reference object for the IT department is no longer application systems or solutions, but rather products. Thus, the IT department's base model must change. The phase oriented internal view, with the distinctive planning, development, and operating phases, is replaced by an integrated product view, which allows customers to be offered complete products. If the business unit's task was primarily specifying system requirements, then it now concentrates on negotiating with the IT service provider over business oriented product characteristics.

2.2.3 Core Concepts and Recommendations

- The collaboration between business units and IT service providers is based on the purchases and sales of IT products.
- IT services are the manufacturing units and IT products are the selling units produced by IT service providers.
- An IT product is made up of IT services and supports a customer's business process or business product.
- An IT product must be of use and advantageous to the customer's business process or business product.
- Two types of IT services can be differentiated: resource oriented services and solution oriented services.
- Two types of IT products can be differentiated: business process supporting and business product supporting products.
- Process supporting IT products are suitable for both the support of standardized business processes with high volumes (e.g. bookkeeping processes, personnel processes, or purchase processes) and individual business processes (e.g. distribution or logistics processes).
- A product oriented information management requires new roles. Product management is of utmost importance because it is responsible for the sales and purchasing of IT products for both the service provider and the customer, respectively.
- An IT service provider's development and production units must work closely together in order to define a customer-fair product portfolio.

2.3 Industrialization of IT Service Production

2.3.1 Context

IT services must be designed and produced by IT service providers. The IT service production can thus be regarded as a manufacturing process, which in many respects is comparable with the manufacturing processes of other companies and industries. Following we will describe some analogies between industrial manufacturing and IT service production. The goal is to identify those areas in which it is possible and makes sense to transfer successful management concepts and methods from industrial manufacturing to IT service production.

2.3.2 IT Service Production

The IT service production can be seen as a manufacturing process. It consists of the three main activities presented in Fig. 16.

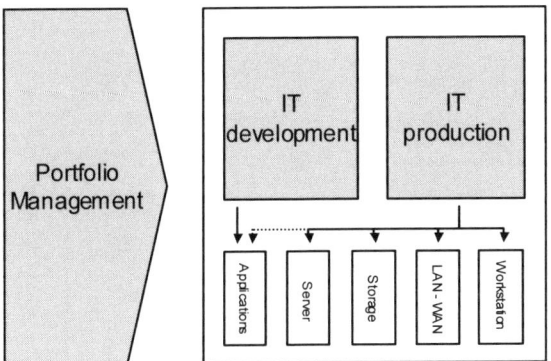

Fig. 16. IT service production process

In the context of Portfolio Management, which is often called program management in industrial manufacturing, the service provider's portfolio of IT services (the manufacturing portfolio) is actively configured and controlled. Portfolio Management specifies the service characteristics and defines requirements for IT development and IT production. Development is responsible for the technical design of services. Within the IT unit, development concentrates predominantly on application development. The production infrastructure of an IT service provider, as previously described in the introduction, consists of five main elements, namely: application systems, servers, memory, WAN/LAN, and workstations. IT production is responsible, with the exception of applications, for the organization of production infrastructure and controls the actual production process. A detailed description of processes and tasks within IT service production is presented in the description of the model of an integrated information management in Chapter 3.

The idea of considering IT service production a manufacturing process permits successful management approaches and methods to be transferred from industrial manufacturing to IT service production.

As a starting point for the transfer it is worthwhile to take a look at the historical development of industrial service production. Fig. 17 presents an overview of the central concepts, drivers, and results, which shaped the development of industrial service production.

Looking at history, two significant insights can be won. First of all, industrial service production was confronted with comparable IT service production challenges: Automation, modularity, focusing, flexibility, and value orientation are core challenges in both industrial and IT service production. Secondly, development within IT service production lags behind.

Today IT service production is dominated by those questions which industrial management considered and had to deal with in the 1980s.

	Concept	Driver	Result
1960s	experience curve	100% greater volume 20-30% lesser costs	big factories
1970s	Portfolio Management	cash input is proportional to growth rate, companies are made up of independent departments	specialized factories
1970s	debt management	"Growth through debt"	automation
1980s	causer incurred costs	complexity, aggressive pricing	production modularity
1980s	restructuring	seeking protection against Corporate Raiders	concentration on core competencies
1990s	time management	"reaction time is everything"	JIT, Kanban, Lean Factory
1990s	common platform	standardization	value networks

Fig. 17. Concepts, drivers, and results in the production of industrial services

The process of service production has opposing goals, namely those of the external market and those of internal operating (see Fig. 18). On the one hand, customers of a company expect a speedy delivery and high quality of products. However, service production is subject to internal operating goals, above all high flexibility, which allow for a quick reaction to changes in demand, and as small as possible operating costs. An economic gain can only be achieved though a combination of both systems.

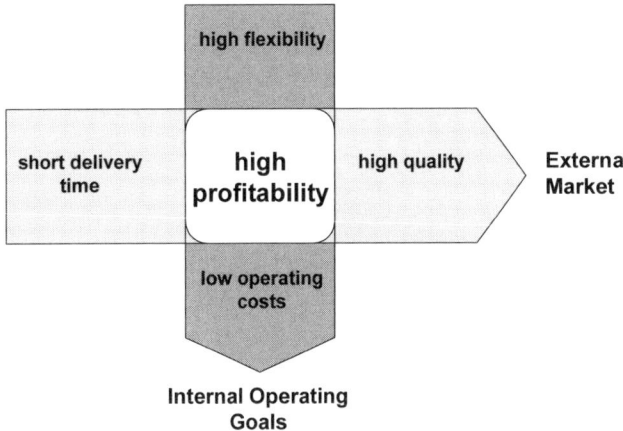

Fig. 18. Divergent goals in the production of IT services

Industrial manufacturing management concepts can be transferred to the production of IT services. From our standpoint such a transfer appears promising, especially within the following five areas (see Fig. 19):

- *Integrated service production* concepts: At the core of these concepts is an integrative, that is, holistic perspective of the service creation process. This includes concepts such as Value Engineering, Design-for-Manufacture-and-Assembly, and Plant Engineering. Value Engineering enables and supports a function oriented and economically efficient process. With respect to the creation of IT products, this means creating in line with demand and competitive IT services. Using the principles of Design-for-Manufacture-and-Assembly, IT services can be designed so that they are geared for production. Geared for production means that services are produced fulfilling all functional requirements but at the same time at minimum cost. Plant Engineering (factory planning) offers solutions for planning and designing manufacturing plants, as well as monitoring the entire production implementation. In IT this refers in particular to planning computing centers.

- *Production planning and controlling* concepts: A number of both detailed and proven concepts are employed in industrial manufacturing in the areas of production program planning, quantity planning, scheduling, capacity planning, and order monitoring. These concepts are clearly more advanced and efficient than those approaches currently used in IT service production.

- *Costing and performance accounting* concepts: These concepts can be employed in resolving fundamental questions of costing and performance calculation (e.g. process cost calculation, accounting of single and overhead costs, or the distinction between use and idle time costs). They can also be used with regard to the concrete design of cost categories, cost centers, and cost object accounting, calculation procedures, product profitability, or plan cost calculations. Industrial manufacturing offers a broad wealth of experience upon which the often rudimentary approaches in IT service production can be built.

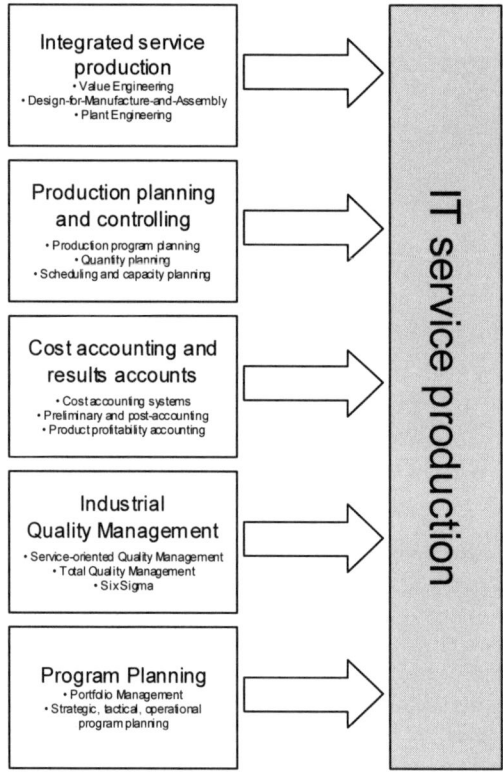

Fig. 19. Analogies between industrial and IT service production

- *Quality Management* concepts: Although quality plays a central role in IT service production, IT Quality Management approaches in practice often exhibit strong phase orientation, for example in software development or operating. A holistic, customer view of quality usually fails to answer even the most fundamental questions, for example questions about systematic definition and recording of the quality costs caused by IT products. Here holistic approaches developed in industrial manufacturing, for example total quality management or Six Sigma offer clearly more far-reaching solution concepts.

- *Program Planning* concepts: Industrial manufacturing has a broad wealth of experience of concepts and methods for the complete planning and controlling of manufacturing and sales programs. Manufacturing and sales programs are planned strategically, tactically, and operationally. Planning is closely interlocked with development and production planning. IT service providers can use this experience to actively arrange and steer their portfolio of IT services.

In the context of integrated information management all five areas enumerated above are evaluated and play a central role in the description of the universal model in Chapter 3. Again in Chapter 4 these areas are described with real sample applications.

2.3.3 Core Concepts and Recommendations

- IT service production is a manufacturing process which consists of the three main activities Portfolio Management, development, and production.

- Successful management approaches and methods from industrial manufacturing and service production can be transferred to IT service production.

- Concepts of integrated manufacturing, production planning and controlling, cost and performance accounting, quality management, and program planning can be transferred from industrial manufacturing to IT service production.

- IT service production goals are in conflict. The conflict between external market goals and those of the internal operation must be resolved.

2.4 Integrated Management of Portfolio, Development, and Production

2.4.1 Context

Only when the three subareas of IT service creation, Portfolio Management, development, and production, are held closely together, can an IT service provider produce in line with demand for services in an economically efficient manner. In the following section we look at this challenge in greater detail and describe which requirements must be differentiated in integrated management of portfolio, development, and production.

2.4.2 Integrated Management

The integration efforts in IT service production must go in two directions:

The management processes in IT service production must be both horizontally and vertically integrated.

More concretely this means (see Fig. 20):

- The horizontal integration concentrates on interfaces between Portfolio Management, IT development, and IT production. The goal is to develop consistent management concepts, which do not focus only on one of the three subareas, but instead treat IT service production as a whole.

- In IT service production vertical integration pushes different levels of operation into the foreground. Strategic, planning, and operational tasks exist in each of the three subareas and cannot be regarded separately. Integration is of crucial importance, especially on a strategic level. An IT service provider's portfolio strategy, development strategy, and production strategy must be coordinated with one another. Chapter 3 considers this matter in greater detail. Development and Production Planning are more or less treated separately, but must also be coordinated with regard to scheduling and resources. On the operational level IT production plays a central role in that it contains the majority of tasks for the production of IT services.

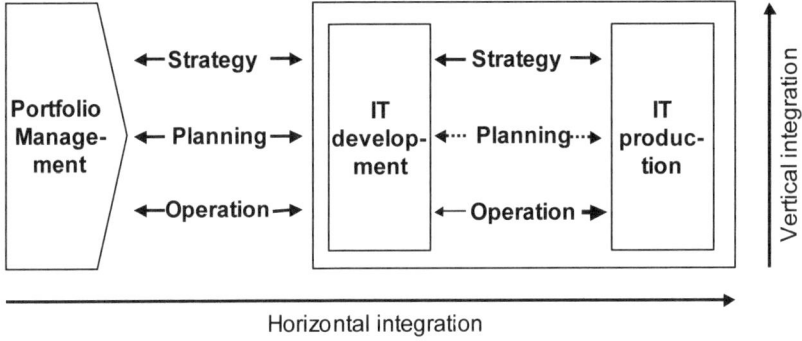

Fig. 20. Horizontal and vertical integration of IT service production

Both integration directions play a central role within the model of the integrated information management that will be introduced in Chapter 3. Considering the status quo situation in IT service production with regard to integration, two deficits come directly to mind:

Today, instead of a whole service portfolio, most individual services are planned, developed, and produced independently. The links between the services create the architectures.

Today, the focus in IT service production is on planning and development, i.e. on the functional organization of IT services. Production plays only a subordinate role.

Long-term improvements can only be achieved by improving information management concepts and instruments. From our standpoint three aspects are center and foremost:

- *Output orientation*: In an output oriented view, outputs of IT service production, i.e. IT services, are centrally positioned. Portfolio Management, development, and production must be regarded as necessary subtasks for the production of a service. All three subtasks must be given equal attention so that a customer oriented, low-priced and qualitatively high-quality IT service can be produced.

- *Consistency*: The majority of information management instruments used today are phase oriented. They concentrate either on Portfolio Management, development, or production. Each phase must be optimized individually. Only consistent, phase-spanning management instruments allow for a total optimization and an output oriented view.

- *Two-way directions*: Today, feedback is usually found only in one of the IT service production phases. Thus, for example, most procedures in software development include loops and feedbacks. However, over more than one phase, a strictly sequential approach is usually pursued. For example, experiences and requirements from production rarely flow into earlier developmental phases. Organizationally, development and production are somewhat consciously separated. Even if processes formally exist for the integration of employees from both production and development teams, in reality they fail frequently due to organizational and psychological barriers. In line with this mindset, in one of our discussions about the typical relationship between development and production, an IT manager put it this way: "The software is developed and then thrown over the wall into production."

IT service providers must face the challenge of a greater integration of portfolio, development, and production tasks.

Production will gain significance within IT service creation.

Production costs represent a great percentage of the total costs of IT service production. It is thus most efficient to work in this area where the largest cost blocks can be effectively reduced. In addition, an increasing product orientation supports this trend. Significant, customer oriented IT products contain a number of production services, which encompass far more than company infrastructure alone. These can only be delivered in the quantity and quality desired by the customer through great efforts in production.

Today's separation of development and production is mirrored in the formal organization of the interface between service providers and customers. The traditional organization of the relationship between the two is presented in Fig. 21 above (Alternative A). The customer makes a request to the development unit, initializing the development of an IT solution. After the solution (fulfilling the request) has been manufactured, the solution is accepted by the customer. Afterwards the customer sends a request to production and hands over the developed solution. It is a purely formal mechanism with which the delivery of the customer's developed solution is passed on to production. In practice the technical delivery is carried out directly between development and production. The consequence of Alternative A for the customer is that he must make two contracts with usually two different contracting parties, which presents an unnecessary complexity to business. Practice shows that problems are often thrown back and forth between development and production, both assuming the other is responsible, which creates great problems for the customer in identifying who the responsible persons actually are. With this alternative, cooperation takes place between service provider and customers based on development and production resources, thus it is particularly suitable for Category 1 (see Chapter 2.2) resource oriented IT services.

Integrated Management of Portfolio, Development, and Production   37

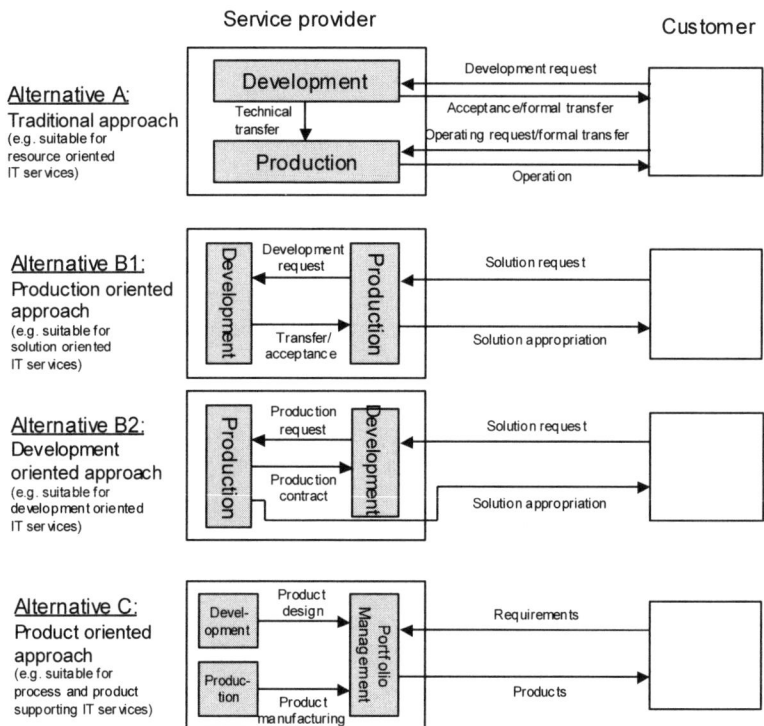

Fig. 21. Organizational alternatives for the formal interfaces between service providers and customers

Alternative B presents an intermediate path in the direction of a strictly product oriented cooperation. From a customer perspective it leads to a reduction of complexity because the customer's interface with the service provider is exclusively with production (Alternative B1) or development (Alternative B2). In the context of Alternative B1, production is responsible for the whole customer relationship. The customer makes a request to production for the delivery of an IT solution. Production then makes a request for solution development and receives the finished solution from the development unit. In this approach a part of the contractual relationship is shifted from the customer to the solution provider, which clearly reduces the complexity for the customer. Alternative B2 illustrates the reverse approach. The development takes on a part of the customer relationship, receives the request for development of an IT solution, and coordinates with production on the contractual conditions of operating. Production provides the customer with an operating solution. Alternatives B1 and B2 are particularly suitable for Category 2 solution oriented IT services.

Alternative C presents the strictly product oriented approach again, which is particularly important when employing business process and business product supporting IT products. The customer buys the service provider's IT products. The interface to the customer comes in the form of Portfolio Management. The IT products contain both development and production services. For this reason both development and production units are equally involved in the organization and production of the services.

In practice how can portfolio, development, and production views be integrated into common perspective?

We see a promising approach in the transfer of integrated management concepts from industrial manufacturing (as previously described) to IT service production.

Simultaneous Engineering, Design-for-Manufacture-and-Assembly, Plant Engineering, or Value Engineering are only a few of the concrete concepts which developed in industrial manufacturing as a result of many years invested in integrative management processes.

2.4.3 Core Concepts and Recommendations

- The management processes within IT service production must be both horizontally and vertically integrated.

- Horizontal integration focuses on the interfaces between Portfolio Management, development, and production. The management processes must be consistently arranged horizontally.

- Vertical integration focuses on the integration of strategic, planning, and operational task levels within IT service production.

- Integrated management processes must be output oriented, consistent, and bi-directional.

- Production must be granted a higher level of priority in IT service production. Production has considerable influence over the quality and manufacturing costs of IT services.

- A service provider must see its service portfolio as a whole, and steer and control it accordingly.

- An IT service provider's customer interface is Portfolio Management and not IT development and production units.

2.5 Life Cycle Oriented Information Management

2.5.1 Context

IT products, like all products, have a life cycle. For this reason a service provider's portfolio of IT products must be life cycle oriented. In this chapter we consider what the effects of IT product life cycles on information management are and what exactly life cycle oriented Portfolio Management means.

2.5.2 Life Cycle Perspectives

Today, many IT service providers are facing a great challenge: Year for year their operation, maintenance, and support costs continue to increase. Despite consolidation and standardization efforts they have not been able to sustain any decline in these cost blocks. This is mainly due to the introduction of new applications and new technologies, platforms, and architectures. It would be possible to, at least partially, compensate the effects of this development in economically speaking "good times" by increasing IT budgets. However there are serious consequences should budgets stagnate or sink. An ever-larger percentage of the budget is needed to keep the existing solutions and infrastructures intact. Fewer and fewer means are available for the realization of new solutions. Today, many IT units complain about the fact that only 10–30% of budgets are allocated to realizing new IT projects. The remainder is spent on maintenance of current production. It is increasingly difficult under these premises for the IT unit to play a formative or strategic role within the company.

Why has this developed as it has? In our view the main reason is the neglect of life cycle oriented management concepts. It is easy to be intuitively clear on the relationships between nonrecurring costs of new IT solution development and recurring costs of existing solution production and enhancement. However, there exist neither whole life cycle models nor concrete numbers and facts regarding life cycle costs. Even today, IT Portfolio Management gives hardly any attention to aspects of the IT life cycle.

> *Life cycle management is a task belonging to Portfolio Management. The portfolio of IT products must be actively designed and controlled with respect to the time/product maturity horizon.*

This problem is most avidly demonstrated when searching for IT life cycle models. IT life cycle models deal almost exclusively with concepts for managing the software development life cycle. Certainly, development is important, but it is only one phase in the life cycle of an IT product. Comprehensive life cycle models, which start with planning and end with retiring the product's operation, are found extremely seldom in information management.

Very gradually service providers are beginning to realize that design decisions, made in the development phase, have great impact on the software's operation and productivity. The well-known relationship between how costs appear and how and when they are determined is also evident in industrial IT products, as shown in Fig. 22.

Decisions made early on in development generate a majority of the subsequent IT product's life cycle costs.

These costs are of particular relevance in the later life cycle phases, i.e. in production. At that point though they can only be marginally influenced.

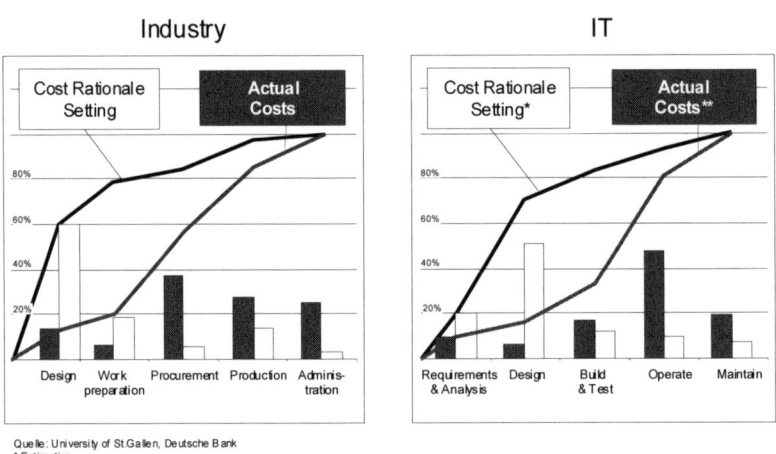

Fig. 22. Cost rationale setting and actual costs in a product's life cycle

In IT this neglected link has resulted in years of exploding production costs, complex infrastructures, and problems in quality. With each new IT solution new systems, platforms, and architectures have been introduced into production. Developments, like the Internet or E-Business, have resulted in completely new production infrastructures. Today, production is confronted with "server chaos," a term coined in one of our discussions by the head of a computing center. It is not surprising that presently due to this development cost oriented topics such as platform consolidation, standardization, adaptability, and virtualization dominate IT production.

IT Product Life Cycles

IT products go through a life cycle. Costs incurred and possible gains of an IT product change as the product goes through the phases of its life cycle. The life cycle of an IT product can be divided into several phases. These can be seen from either a service provider's or market perspective.

The manufacturer oriented product life cycle is based on the typical life cycle phases of an information system and is presented in Fig. 23. It begins with a planning and an initial development phase. The initial development phase covers not only real development but also integration and testing. At the end of the initial development phase, product production begins. This phase includes the actual operating of production infrastructure, for example server, application systems and networks, product support (most importantly user support), and continuous maintenance. While operating, products are also simultaneously being enhanced. In contrast to maintenance, which concentrates on the elimination of errors, product enhancement incorporates new customer requirements and functional extensions. The last phase of the IT product life cycle is retirement of operation or decommission. In a closer examination of each phase, actual tasks can be assigned to each life cycle phase. These assignments will be handled later in Chapter 4.3, where the distribution of tasks will be discussed using a practical example.

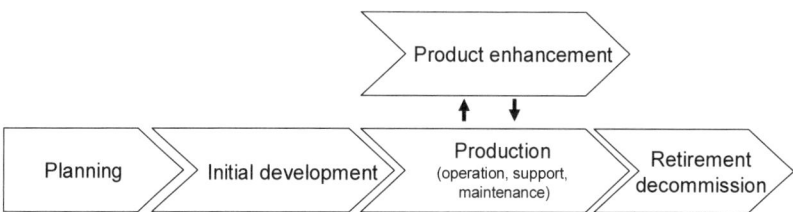

Fig. 23. The service provider's view of the IT product life cycle

Comparable manufacturer oriented life cycle models exist. As an example, the Business Application Life Cycle developed by Gartner Research is presented in Example 4.

Manufacturing oriented life cycle perspectives allow for the development of holistic product management concepts. Using these concepts, however, little can be said about a product's marketability. For a service provider this is of utmost importance, particularly if it concerns the strategic adjustment of its product portfolio. For this reason market focused life cycle models play an important role in IT.

Ex. 4. Business Application Life Cycle by Gartner Research [Zrimsek et al. 2003]

The introduction of new IT applications is, in practice, often considered a nonrecurring project, which is finished with the start-up of application. The Business Application Life Cycle developed by Gartner Research replaces this project oriented view with a life cycle orientation. The Business Application Life Cycle concentrates on the life cycle of purchased software applications.

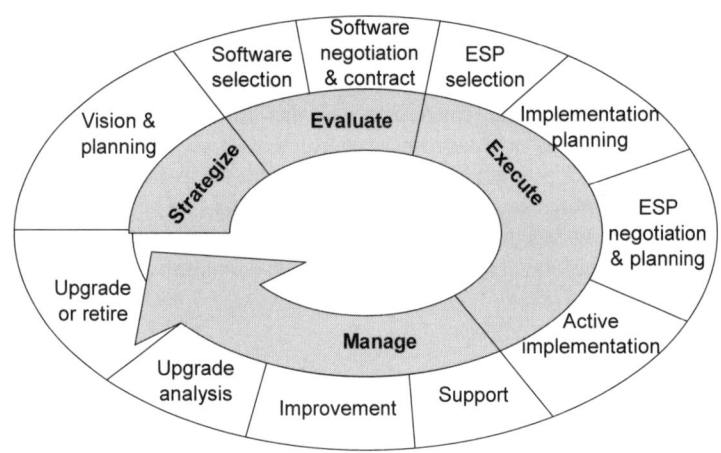

Fig. 24. Business Application Life Cycle

The Business Application Life Cycle has four core phases as presented in Fig. 24: Strategize, Evaluate, Execute, and Manage. Tasks are specified and assigned to each phase.

The goal of the Strategize Phase is to plan the future business and technology initiatives. The Evaluate Phase results in the acquisition of an IT application which fulfills the requirements of the respective business process. This model focuses on purchased IT applications, thus essential elements of evaluation include the selection of suppliers and the negotiation and signing of a contract. The Execute Phase covers all tasks which are necessary for the implementation of an IT application. The specified activities must not necessarily run simultaneously. All tasks taking place after the implementation are part of the Manage phase. In addition to training, support, and controlling, this also includes functionality and technology improvement as well as the final disengagement of the IT application.

The traditional market oriented life cycle of a product typically differentiates between the phases of product development, product introduction, product growth, product maturity, and product decline as presented in Fig. 25. The possible revenue and profit of a product depends on which life cycle phase the product is actually in. A service provider must thus have product replacements at hand at the end of a current market life cycle. It must also strive to have a balanced product portfolio, with products in different life cycle phases.

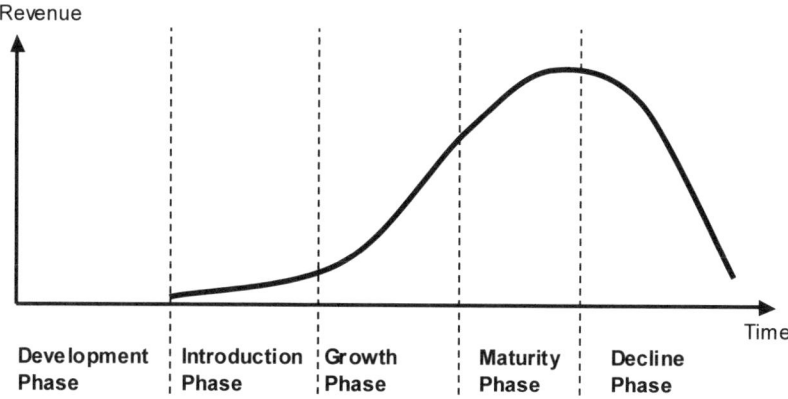

Fig. 25. Classical market oriented product life cycle

In each life cycle phase the service provider's product management faces different challenges [Matys 2002]:·

- In the product's *Development Phase* it must be ready for the market as quickly as possible, but appropriate measures must also be taken for the introduction to the market.
- In the *Introduction Phase*, the identification and elimination of a new product's "teething pains" stands in the foreground with the product's market establishment and reaching the breakeven point.
- The consolidation of product growth is the main goal of the *Growth Phase*. This can take place, for example, by way of an increase in product quality and/or product functionality.
- In the *Maturity Phase* the goal is to defend the product's market position, for example, by using differentiation strategies, price reductions, new channels of distribution, or intensified sales promotion initiatives. Already in this phase the development of a successor product should begin.
- The main objective of this *Decline Phase* is to avoid losses. The product must be taken off the market in a timely manner and replaced by a successor.

Independent of whether a manufacturing- or market-focused life cycle perspective is taken, life cycle orientation directly affects information management. Acting as examples, three consequences are discussed here:

- *Within Portfolio Management, expected life cycle costs of an IT product must already be carefully considered* and flow into product evaluation and prioritization. In practice, today, decisions about IT portfolios are usually made on the basis of IT development costs.

- *Different development alternatives for an IT product must be evaluated with regard to their effects on the entire product life cycle.* In particular, consequences for future production must be considered. Decisions made in the development phase, for example the choice of certain system platforms or application architectures, will have a great impact on later production. Developers must be aware of this and ideally be given a set of rules, which points out the effects of certain decisions on the life cycle.

- *IT product controlling must be made on the basis of life cycle costs.* Only with this information can economical decisions be made as to the point of an IT solution's retirement or a complete cost/benefit analysis be made.

In IT special attention must be given to the strong interdependency of IT products. Between the products there exists a multiplicity of dependences and interfaces, which must be considered in a life cycle management context. Thus, for example, an IT product which has reached the end of its life cycle sometimes cannot be stopped and/or taken out of operation, because the application systems used for this product are needed for the production of other products.

Product Data Management (PDM)

Precise and reliable information about a product in each phase of its life cycle is a prerequisite for life cycle management. It is the task of PDM to collect and manage this information and to make it accessible. In the 1980s, in industrial manufacturing, the term PDM was coined for tools with which CAD files and designs were organized and managed. Since then PDM has gradually developed and today forms the basis of a company wide management of product life cycles. PDM is incorporated in the planning phase of a product, where all product relevant information is collected. The collected information includes not only descriptive electronic documents, such as designs, documentations, or marketing plans, but also information about the product itself, such as product structure, product parts or necessary raw materials, information about current product status, and workflow relevant information, such as data from project management.

The collected PDM information can be evaluated at different levels of aggregation. For example, highly consolidated information about products is an important basis for managerial decisions. In contrast, product developers need rather detailed information about product structure to get their work done. One of PDM's goals is to collect and assemble information just once and make it available for different information processing systems, such as a development environment or text processing system.

The introduction of advanced PDM tools led to a clear shortening of information access times and reduced redundancy in industry. In order to obtain these positive effects also in IT, it is necessary to introduce and utilize PDM as an instrument in information management. Here existing sources of information, which have been made available in the context of Asset Management or Configuration Management, can partially be taken advantage of. However, information here is usually not sufficient for PDM, as shown in Fig. 26.

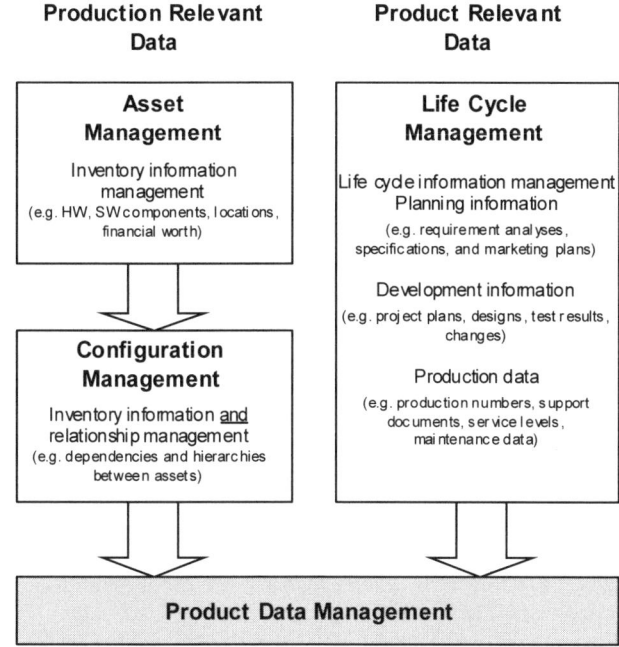

Fig. 26. IT Product Data Management (PDM)

A company's IT tangible assets are accounted for in its inventory within the framework of Asset Management. These IT tangible assets include, for example, elements of hardware infrastructure (like servers, workstation systems, printers, routers, or cabling), software elements (like application systems or software licenses), and documentation. In addition to the asset's fundamental information, financial information, such as current write-off value, can also be collected.

The inventory data created by Asset Management gives little information about the relationships and interdependencies between the individual elements. Practically, however, it is exactly this information that is of significance. For example, if a network component is replaced or if a new release of software is introduced, then the effects of these changes must be anticipated and planned for in time. A supporter should be able to recognize interdependencies between individual infrastructure elements in order to analyze the effects and causes of an error. Configuration Management is the commonly known name given to those responsible for managing the relationships between components described by Asset Management. Example 5 shows, in practice, how such a configuration management can be designed based on the IT Infrastructure Library (ITIL, see Chapter 2.6).

> **Ex. 5.** Configuration Management based on ITIL [OGC 2000]
>
> Concerning ITIL, Configuration Management is responsible for the description of a logical model of the entire infrastructure and all services. It is the basis for all the other defined support processes in ITIL: Incident Management, Problem Management, Change Management, and Release Management.
>
> Configuration Management is built upon a Configuration Management Database (CMDB). Specifications described in CMDB are stored as Configuration Items (CI). Typical CIs are hardware components, system software, application systems, standard software, databases, platforms, software releases, change documentation, network components or service management components, like capacity plans, incidents reports, or change requests. Each company must individually define the level of detail at which CIs are defined. ITIL suggests, complementary to the CMDB, that a Definite Software LIBRARY (DSL) should be installed, in which all official software CIs are physically kept, for example, all original copies of software installed at the company.
>
> Each CI is described by attributes. Typical attributes are name, serial number, category, version number, location, owner, license, status, relations, incidents, problems, or changes. Meanwhile there are a number of professional software solutions available for the construction of a CMDB and administration of CIs.

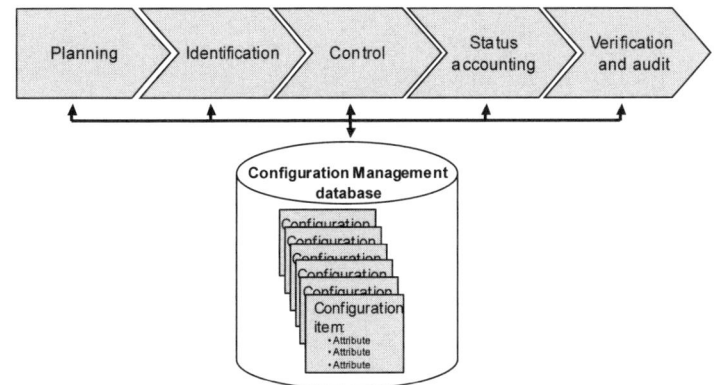

Fig. 27. Configuration Management process and database

ITIL suggests five fundamental activities for the construction of a Configuration Management:

- *Planning*: Definition of goals, scope, rules, guidelines, and procedures of Configuration Management.
- *Identification*: Selection and identification of configuration structure of all CIs.
- *Control*: Assurance of fitting and suitability of CIs; only authorized and identifiable CIs may be taken into the CMDB.
- *Status accounting*: Preparation of information on each CI's current and historical data over its entire life cycle.
- *Verification and audit*: Implementation of controls and audits to examine and verify the physical existence of all CIs and their correct registration in the CMDB.

If Configuration Management is to manage IT product information, then the relationships between business and technical information must also be described. In addition to actual product information, product structure information is also very important, i.e. the individual IT services making up the product, and the infrastructure required for the production of the services. Fig. 28 presents an example of product information to be registered in the context of Configuration Management.

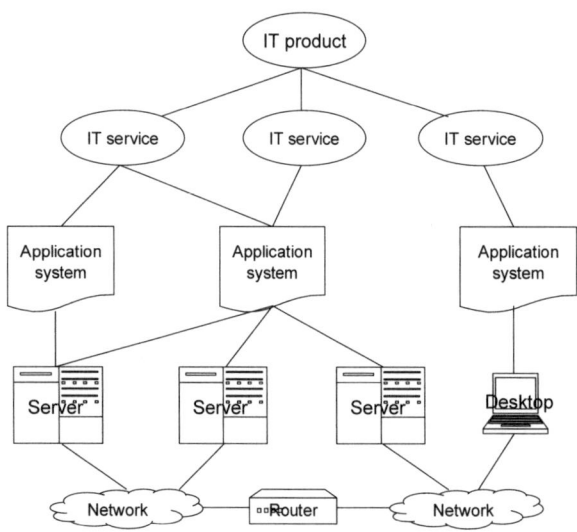

Fig. 28. Product information within Configuration Management

PDM goes beyond Configuration Management, and requires the collection of product related, life cycle oriented information. Here all information relevant to the individual life cycle phases of a product is significant.

In a product's planning phase, for example, requirement analyses are made, functionalities are specified, or business cases are calculated. In the case of a new development, there exists a good deal of development relevant information about the product's required IT services (e.g. service designs, service versions, source code documentation, or test results). Project management information should also be registered in the context of PDM, for example, project plans, assigned resources, and financial information. In the development of an IT service, if external services are bought, then information about the purchase process is also to be entered. This includes, for example, offers, contracts, or guarantee conditions. Even within the production phase there exists a multitude of information. Examples here are SLAs, support and servicing contracts, or an error history.

2.5.3 Core Concepts and Recommendations

- Portfolio Management must be life cycle oriented.
- Every IT product goes through a life cycle, which must be energetically designed and followed.

- Decisions made in the early phases of a product's life cycle have a major impact on later life cycle phases. This applies in particular to decisions which are made during development and which have a significant influence on quality and production costs.
- In Portfolio Management the expected life cycle costs of an IT product must be taken into consideration.
- The cost related evaluation and prioritization of IT products must be based on life cycle costs.
- A product's various development alternatives are to be analyzed with regard to their effect on the product's life cycle and, in particular, on production.
- PDM enables consistent and precise product information to be collected and evaluated through each phase of its life cycle.
- PDM can build upon existing data within Asset Management and Configuration Management. It is then possible to complement this information with product related data.

2.6 Standard Information Management Processes

2.6.1 Context

Based upon experience made in other business units, information management units are gradually recognizing the gains to be made by employing standard processes as a means of process optimization and cost reduction. Operational processes are already often tool supported and standardized, for example, in company computing centers or software development. The positive effects of this process uniformity are gradually being applied to other information management processes, which are to be analyzed for a possible standardization. In this chapter we present two models, ITIL and COBIT, both with a broad base of support in practice. ITIL and COBIT are both used to design standardized IT management processes.

2.6.2 Reference Models

In many business areas standardized processes have established themselves through the installation and use of standard software solutions such as SAP R/3. In most companies, for example, finance, controlling, personnel, and purchasing processes are designed and organized almost identically. In IT this is true only marginally. First of all it is not common to think of IT efforts as processes. Instead

IT unit work allocation is primarily function oriented. Communication between the functional units is difficult, even though the production of customer oriented products necessarily requires an overall function-spanning cooperation. In addition, the prevalent view still exists that IT processes should not be standardized. There are many unique company characteristics to be considered and any standardization would be accompanied by a loss of strategic, competitive advantages. For this reason processes today are usually designed individually and only somewhat standardized for information system planning, development, and production despite the availability of reference models.

The advantages of process standardization have not yet been realized in IT. Only rudimentary versions of transparent documentation exist covering all IT processes and their relationships. This hampers a focused, structured modification when conditions change. A company-wide benchmarking is also more difficult.

> *Several reference models and Best Practices exist, which can be used in designing information management processes. Those most applicable and of greatest importance can be found especially in service oriented approaches.*

Service oriented models bring together many elements of product orientation, as previously discussed. These models provide tips and hints as to which management processes are required for an efficient development and provision of customer oriented IT products. Fig. 29 presents an overview of current service oriented models. ITIL and COBIT will be explained in greater detail due to their particular practical relevance.

IT Infrastructure Library (ITIL)

In the mid-1980s English governmental authorities challenged the efficiency and effectiveness of IT services to such an extent that an initiative was started calling for the documentation and standardization of IT service production processes. Based on this initiative, the Central Computer and Telecommunications Agency (CCTA) of the British government (which has since become a sub-unit of the Office of Government Commerce) has been involved in the development of a process oriented collection of Best Practices for planning, monitoring, and controlling IT services (in cooperation with IT specialists, computing center operators, and advisors). The consistent service orientation of IT service providers is the main thrust of ITIL. IT services must be defined on the basis of customer requirements, and IT service providers' associated internal processes must be aligned accordingly. ITIL is continuously developed and updated by commercial practice representatives, in particular by users, manufacturers, and advisors.

> *ITIL has developed into the international de facto standard for IT service providers. ITIL is a producer-independent collection of Best Practices for an IT service provider's design and organization of management processes.*

Model	Author	Description
Public Domain		
ITIL	OGC	De facto standard for service oriented IT management
COBIT	ISACA	Standard for auditing and controlling IT management
MNM Service Model	University of Munich	Generic model for the definition of service related articulation, concepts, and structure rules
IT Service CMM	Vrije Universiteit	Maturity model for IT service management
Managerial Step-by-Step Plan (MSP)	Delft University of Technology	Incremental plan for IT management design
Non Public Domain		
ASL	Pink Roccade	Reference model for application management
BIOOlogic	HIT	Object oriented model for IT management
HP IT Service Reference Model	HP	Based on ITIL, a process model for IT management
IPW	Quint Wellington Redwood	First ITIL based process model for IT service management
Integrated Service Management (ISM)	KPN & BHVB	IT management design approach as a system integrator
IBM IT Process Model	IBM	ITIL based process model for IT management
Perform	Cap Gemini Ernst & Young	ITIL based management standard for business information delivery
Microsoft Operations Framework (MOF)	Microsoft	ITIL based and Microsoft environment norm process model for IT management
Standard Integrated Management Approach (SIMA)	Interprom	Approach for designing management and security aspects of open, multivendor IT infrastructures

Fig. 29. Overview of service oriented reference models

This is the foundation for the International IT Service Management Forum (ITSMF) with at present over 2000 partner companies. ITIL is made up of the five core modules presented in Fig. 30: The module Business Perspective covers the strategic elements of IT service management, such as IT alignment or relationship management. Service Delivery deals with planning, monitoring, and controlling IT services, with respect to service delivery. Service Support deals with the implementation of service processes and user support. The management of applications over entire life cycles is dealt with in Application Management. The ICT Infrastructure Management is concerned with all aspects of infrastructure management, from the design and planning phases through to realization, and including operation and technical support.

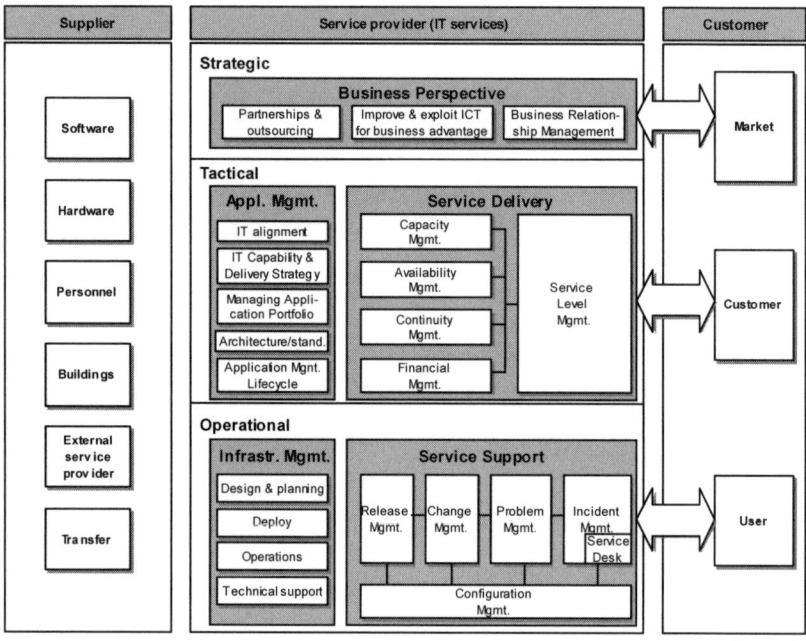

Fig. 30. IT Infrastructure Library (ITIL) modules

Practically speaking, the most important modules are "service delivery" and "service support." They form the actual core of ITIL. An overview of these modules is presented below:

- *Service Level Management:* Service Level Management represents the customer interface and guarantees an efficient and effective CRM in the sense of a "one face to the customer" approach. Negotiation, agreement, and monitoring are central to SLAs. In an iterative process based on customer requirements IT services, which are to be supplied, are defined in a service level structure. In coordination with the customer, different quality criteria are to be considered and agreed upon. There are further consequences of Service Level Management. The levels imply that the service provider's production and/or procurement process, which is aligned by internal Operational Level Agreements

(OLAs), and supplier-related Underpinning Contracts (UCs) are defined so that the corresponding customer SLA can be guaranteed. Finally, the agreed upon SLA, OLA, and UC must be continuously monitored. Should a breach of contract loom, improvement measures must be initiated. Furthermore, a constant reporting of service degree grading must be institutionalized. This reporting must address both management and customers.

- *Capacity Management*: Capacity Management secures the required provision and monitoring of demanded capacities. Business, service, and resource oriented capacities must be differentiated. The task of business oriented Capacity Management is to forecast, plan, and implement in a timely manner customers' future business requirements with respect to IT services. Capacity requirement expectations can be derived from business plans for new services, service improvements, or plans for growth. Analysis of current rates of utilization can be used for decisions on measures for capacity extending or downsizing. For individual services the capacity necessary for the agreed upon service level must be monitored. This is a service oriented Capacity Management task. As a final point, capacity management, in a resource oriented framework, must supervise and evaluate rates of utilization of individual components (e.g. server, networks, etc.) at an operational level.

- *Availability Management*: While Capacity Management is concerned with capacity related interests of IT service providers, Availability Management is responsible for availability relevant interests. It must ensure that customer requirements are met with regard to the availability of IT infrastructure, services, and support organization, and that the service provider can guarantee and sustain this availability with the lowest possible costs. The degree of availability depends on the reliability and maintenance of the IT infrastructure, as well as the effectiveness of the IT support organization. Availability requirements are derived from the Service Level Management defined SLA. These are integrated in internal processes and, when necessary, appropriate measures for increased availability are suggested.

- *IT Service Continuity Management:* The mission of IT Service Continuity Management is it to re-establish services should the system crash. The services must be accessible within a time frame accepted by the customer before the crash, and bypass measures must be made available. A rigorous re-establishment regulation must be made specifically for critical business services. Financial and reputation losses caused by the crash can be evaluated through a Business Impact Analysis. With the results of this analysis, conditions necessary to fulfill minimum requirements are set. In using this information, risk can be analyzed and a Business Continuity Strategy prepared and implemented. An operational controlling must constantly supervise and improve the Continuity Process.

- *Financial Management:* Financial Management is responsible for a financial portrait of the IT service provider's business situation. It contributes to the creation of transparency and efficiency. The Financial Management processes correspond to those of business accounting systems and cover service budgeting, controlling, and accounting. With respect to budgeting, financial means are allocated to the individual units within IT. Controlling realizes an excise fair cost structure for IT service provision and enables, for example, cost–benefit analyses. The structure for service accounting strongly depends on the IT service provider's organizational form. The differences between cost center, profit center, and service center organizations are apparent. Costs, costs plus profit margin, or market prices are charged accordingly.

- *Incident Management*: The following processes are part of service support. They describe the tasks necessary for the operational implementation of support processes. Incident Management's most important task is acceptance, first support, and classification of IT related problems or inquiries. The Service Desk is the user interface. It receives inquiries (Service Requests) and problems (Disturbances). In an initial step these contacts are analyzed, classified, and, if possible, immediately supported. For an efficient organization of this process a "Known Error" database is advantageous. This database stores all problems known to date and appropriate for solution proposals. If problems are new, they are then passed on according to their classification to those responsible for 2nd-level support. Although the further analysis and solution are the duties of Problem Management, it is Incident Management's job to secure that users are informed on the current status of the problem solution process.

  For many companies Incident Management presents the first real contact with ITIL. ITIL projects are usually initiated with the introduction of ITIL compliant Incident Management and Service Desks. Example 2 describes the results of a typical project scenario.

- *Problem Management:* Problem Management is responsible for the solution and correction of IT related disturbances. A significant factor for success is a clean interface to incident management. Problem Management is responsible for disturbance analysis and correction. Here many methods are available, for example, the Kepner and Tregoe analysis, the Ishikawa diagram, or flowchart methods. It is also the duty of problem management to actively invent measures to avoid disturbances. To this end trend analyses are made, which contribute to potential problem identification. Furthermore, a consistent control of the problem solution process and a continuous reporting are necessary in order to increase efficiency within the Problem Management process. When an error is found during problem analysis or diagnosis, a Request for Change (RFC) must be submitted, which then triggers the execution of a problem correction process in the context of a standardized Change Management.

Ex. 6: Introduction of an ITIL compliant Service Desk at T-Mobile Deutschland GmbH [Hochstein et al. 2004]

T-Mobile Germany was confronted with many challenges in the area of IT support. There was no central Hotline structure. Instead each location had a regional Hotline and offered regional on-site support. The support processes grew historically, which led to little standardization, a strong system orientation, and no spanning organizational design. There was no system-supported classification of support inquiries, and no distinction was made between disturbance collection (Incident Management) and disturbance analysis (Problem Management). Although customer opinion polls showed high customer satisfaction in support services, it was primarily due to the personal relations between supporters and customers as well as unbureaucratic cooperation. It was nonetheless lacking transparency in costs, services, and quality, and thus could not be controlled. Moreover, the quality of support was strongly dependent on the supporter and thus was subject to great fluctuations.

For these reasons it was decided to create an ITIL compliant central Service Desk, which should serve as the single point of contact for all support inquiries and disturbance reports. The fundamental distinction between Incident Management and Problem Management was made according to ITIL. Services to be provided were agreed upon on the basis of SLAs and supervised by way of monitoring and reporting processes. In introducing the Service Desk, a new system landscape, made up of two ITIL compliant tools, was implemented (see Fig. 31). With this construction the cooperation between 1st-, 2nd-, and 3rd-level support, as well as between central and decentralized support units was, for the most part, automated.

Critical success factors apparent in the course of the project were an early, active integration of Service Desk customers, an open, partnering cooperation, a dynamic communication, a holistic view of the ITIL processes, and a strict project management. It was demonstrated that with the new structure numerous advantages were now within reach. Through the definition of SLAs, services existed with quality criteria and transparent cost structures. Common market indicators, like the accessibility of service desks, solution quotes, or operating interruption time, were now quantifiable in detail due to the new monitoring process. The centralization led to uniform process and quality standards. The flow of information directed toward customers was able to be noticeably improved. The measurable increase in efficiency was also of importance and was mainly due to the centralization of tasks. However, these benefits were achieved, at least partially, at the expense of individual customer service. Thus, some customers expressed their discontent over the more impersonal organization of the central 1st-level support, which they considered subjectively a reduction in quality.

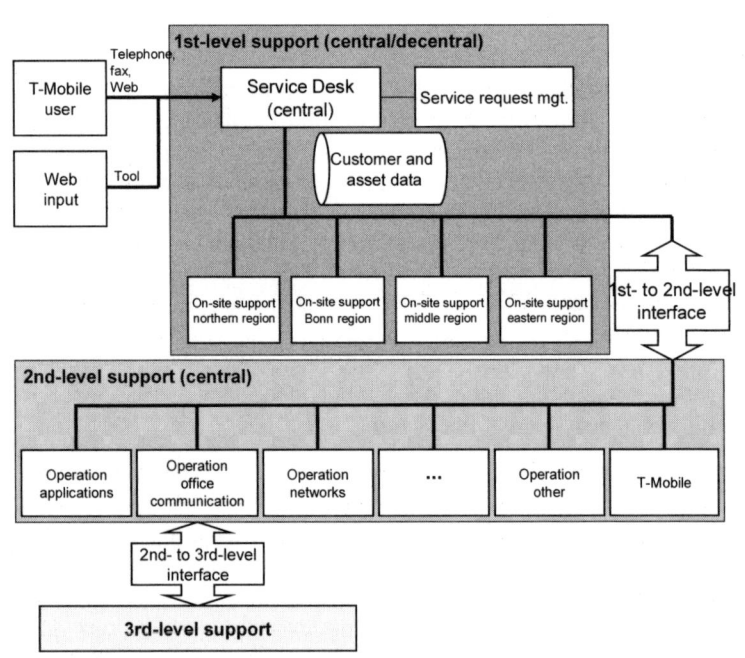

Fig. 31. Process and system landscape after the introduction

A detailed description of this project and project results can be found in Hochstein et al. 2004 or Zarnekow et al. 2005.

- *Change Management:* Change Management plays a central role in ITIL because decisions on internal changes are made here. ITIL gives very exact instructions. ITIL describes what aspects Change Management should concentrate on. ITIL specifies how the organizational implementation should take place and what tasks are necessary for this implementation. Change Management guarantees that changes on tactical or operational levels take place in the context of a standardized Change Management process and under consistent Change Management control. When technology relevant changes are made, then appropriate RFCs must be submitted, which run through a standardized process, beginning with registration and classification over authorization, implementation, and evaluation. Classification here means that RFCs must be prioritized with respect to their importance, costs, and urgency. Depending upon their priority RFCs are streamlined through different processes. For changes with a greater importance, a Change Advisory board (CAB) will be summoned. This CAB is made up of representatives from customers, users, and possibly developers, technical advisors, service staff, and suppliers. The CAB authorizes the RFC. In special cases even the management board may be consulted for authorizing an RFC.

- *Release Management*: The task of Release Management is to assure the successful rollout of software and hardware releases. The first step is to set up Release Policy: all significant roles and responsibilities are defined within its framework. Subsequently, a planning, design, and build process follows, which is closely related to the Release Policy. In this process the crucial components of the release are planned and developed. After a comprehensive test the rollout is planned and executed. During the entire process it is to be ensured that the new components are in alignment with the DSL and the Configuration Database (CMDB). In the DSL all the official versions of all software components are secured. The CMDB was already mentioned in Example 5. In Release Management it is important to pay special attention to an effective interface to Change Management and Configuration Management, so that a more systematic, controlled, and documented change procedure can be adhered to.

- *Configuration Management:* Configuration Management serves as the basis of control of IT infrastructure and IT services. A logical model of infrastructure and services is defined in which Configuration Items (CIs) are identified, controlled, maintained, and verified. The practical tasks of Configuration Management were described previously in Example 5.

ITIL Potential and Limitations

ITIL presents IT service providers with a number of Best Practice descriptions and references for designing standardized, service oriented management processes. However, in order to understand and position ITIL within the full context of information management, the following points should be considered:

- *At present ITIL is of practical importance mainly in operational service support and partially in service delivery*. These two modules form, also from an historical perspective, the core content of the descriptions. Companies receive many very clear instructions as to what must be considered during the implementation of support and delivery processes. The other model components—Application Management, Infrastructure Management, and Business Perspective—offer however only marginal differences in value compared to other models and concepts. These components provide more or less general knowledge in an ITIL form. In practice, they have not found much recognition. For this reason ITIL should be seen not as comprehensive model for the organization of information management, but instead as a collection of Best Practices, which supply valuable references in selected subareas, particularly in service support (see Chapter 4.5).

- *The ITIL is not a process model, but a collection of Best Practices.* It does not provide a consistent process description. Thus, descriptions of input/output, for example, are often missing, which would facilitate a comprehensive understanding of the relationships between processes and the derivations of workflows. With respect to both structure and degree of detail, great differences are to be found in the various model components. Moreover, inconsistencies can be found with regard to the indication of success factors, key data indicators. Even the depth in which individual subareas and activities are described varies greatly.

- *ITIL concentrates on a description of "what must be done to implement service oriented management processes."* How the implementation should be carried out is hardly considered. Since its original publication an additional ITIL volume has been published, and in it a procedural model for the implementation of IT service management is described. However, first of all this model concentrates on the service support topic and, secondly, it is gives only a general description. Companies wanting to redesign their processes on the basis of ITIL therefore receive hardly any concrete suggestions on how the necessary reengineering and change management processes should progress. Here valuable assistance can be offered by commercial model suppliers, whose models are based on ITIL but who supply valuable support and concentrate intentionally on implementation procedures.

- *ITIL is a generic model and contains no industry- or company-specific instructions or references.* The Best Practices described in ITIL can be adapted and applied to many different areas due to their generic description, however each individual company must make this adaptation. ITIL contains little to no regard for industry specific characteristics, and just as few special remarks for small, medium, or large companies.

Control Objectives for Information and Related Technology (COBIT)

The reference model COBIT defines 34 critical IT processes and concentrates particularly on the description of control goals for these processes.

> *COBIT provides a framework for the design organization of IT governance in a company.*

ISACA (Information Systems Audit and Control Association) and IT Governance Institutes have worked on COBIT development since 1993. Meanwhile a third version has been published [ISACA 2004]. It includes a number of national and international standards dealing with quality, security, qualification, and regulatory adherence. In its current version COBIT describes 34 central IT processes, divided into four domains (see Fig. 32). Each process defines a set of business goals, which should be supported by the process. Correspondingly these processes define between three and 30 control goals, which, in the sense of Best Practices, support the supervision of fulfilling the business goals.

Although COBIT is not an official standard in information management, in practice it is relatively widespread. Actually COBIT's standing has been secured by the increasing importance of initiatives with respect to corporate governance, for example in connection with the institutionalization of the Sarbanes Oxley Act. COBIT is a suitable reference model to implement such initiatives in IT units. ISACA, who is responsible for the continual enhancement of COBIT, makes sure that the model is in line with ITIL. As a result COBIT is used frequently, in practice, in combination with ITIL. Practically speaking, this combination enables processes converted on the basis of ITIL to be controlled and tested with COBIT support.

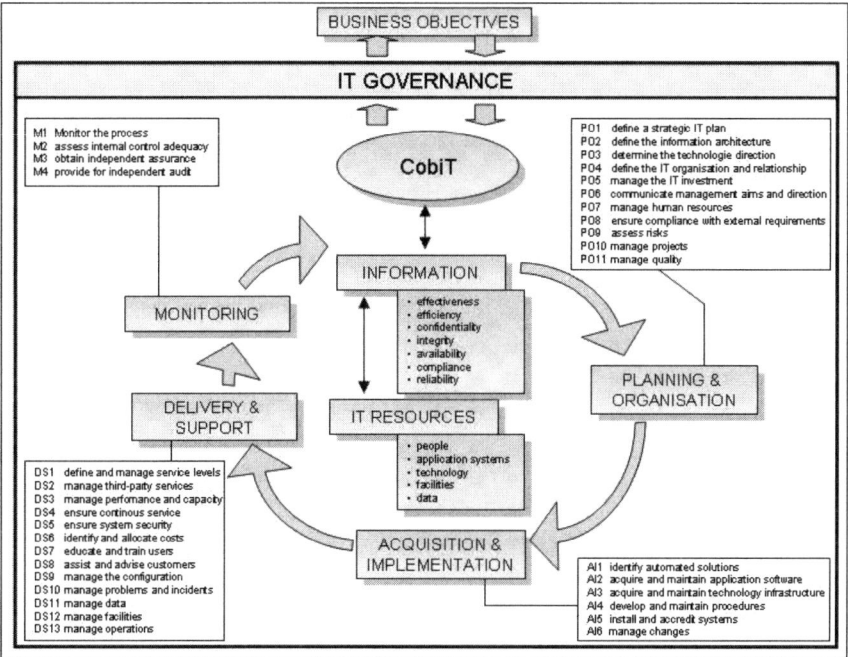

Fig. 32. COBIT reference model

COBIT sets itself apart from all other models by way of its thorough consistency in its representation of the individual processes. Goal definitions, success factors, efficiency, and effectiveness criteria are uniformly formulated for each process. The extensive detail in which processes are described is homogeneous. Unfortunately neither input/output process views are made, nor are definitive management instruments specified, making a clear understanding of process relations murky.

How to proceed with the conversion of activities remains unclear within the individual processes. Also the assignment of responsibilities and competencies is difficult due to vague descriptions of roles. For the real implementation of this model COBIT supplies its own implementation tool set and a maturity model, which allows organizations to assign each process a level of maturity and to identify suitable measures for reaching higher maturity levels. Despite its degree of detail, COBIT remains a generic model, which can be adapted to various situations.

2.6.3 Core Concepts and Recommendations

- Existing reference models and Best Practices can be used to design and organize information management processes. Above all, service oriented models are particularly advantageous.
- IT Infrastructure Library (ITIL) has developed into the international de facto standard for IT service providers and contains a multiplicity of Best Practices for IT service management.
- At present ITIL is of practical value only in the areas of service support and service delivery.
- ITIL's strengths lie in subjects dealing with operational processes.
- ITIL is a collection of Best Practices, not a process model.
- ITIL is a generic model and must be adapted to the individual situation of an IT service provider.
- COBIT is a framework for the organization of IT governance. It sets itself apart through its incisive formalization and its thorough consistency in the representation of 34 critical information management processes.

2.7 Summary

The developments and challenges described in this chapter enable us to identify the central components of a future oriented information management. Recapitulating, these components can be characterized as follows:

- A clear interface must exist between IT service providers and IT customers, which is based on market mechanisms. Portfolio Management takes on the pivotal task of coordinating offers and demands made by IT service providers and IT customers, respectively.

Summary

- IT products must form the basis of the relationship between IT service providers and service customers. An IT product must support a service customer's business process or a business product and be of benefit. IT products are made up of many individual IT services.

- The IT service production process is to be designed and organized in a similar fashion to that of an industrial manufacturing process. It consists of the three main activities: Portfolio Management, development, and production. From the broad wealth of experience in industrial manufacturing, there are especially important concepts which lend themselves to IT service production. In particular, they are the concepts dealing with integrated service production, production planning and steering, cost and performance accounting, quality management, and program planning.

- The methods and instruments used for managing IT service production must be integrated, i.e. output oriented, consistent, and bi-directional. The integration must be both horizontal (i.e. concentrating on interfaces between Portfolio Management, development, and production) and vertical (i.e. in light of strategic, planning, and operational levels of action).

- Portfolio Management must be life cycle oriented. IT products must be proactively managed over their entire life cycles. Special attention must be given to the interdependencies between development and production. Decisions made in the development phase of an IT product have a real impact on the chronologically later production phase, and above all on production costs.

- In designing and organizing information management processes, existing reference models, like ITIL or COBIT, should be taken into account.

The model of an integrated information management presented in the following chapter incorporates these components and shows how they can be combined into a comprehensive management model for IT service providers.

3 Integrated Information Management

3.1 Model Overview: From Plan–Build–Run to Source–Make–Deliver

The fundamental and well-known concepts and models used in information management are only suitable for the challenges described in the previous section to a limited degree. This applies especially to the Plan–Build–Run approach, which for many years has served, in practice, as the basis for designing process and workflow management structures in information management. In our opinion the strict adherence to the Plan–Build–Run approach is one of the main causes of a lack of effectiveness and efficiency in many IT units. This approach imposes a modus operandi, which unconditionally divides a company's IT activities into an unending sequence of projects to modify IT services. Consequently, too little attention is paid to the costs and quality of current service portfolios.

The integrated information management (IIM) model presented below offers an answer to the challenges described in the previous chapter. It describes the central management processes of an IT service provider which are necessary for the production and use of IT products. In addition, the customer interface is also described, in particular with regard to customer processes in purchasing IT products.

The IIM model is based on the following fundamental assumptions. These assumptions are based on the building block components identified in the preceding chapter.

- There exists a customer supplier relationship between the service provider and its customers, in which transactions are made in internal company or external markets.
- All service exchanges and transactions are based on IT products.
- IT service production is to be thought of as an integrated manufacturing process.
- The management of IT products is based on life cycle based management concepts.
- Established reference models for information management are taken into account. This is especially important when considering service oriented models.

The SCOR Model as the Foundation of an Integrated Information Management

IT service providers and service customers are two elements in the production and use of IT services value creation and supply chain. It thus seems obvious to design and organize tasks within information management on the basis of established reference models for Supply Chain Management (SCM). The model for integrated information management is based on the SCOR (Supply Chain Operations Reference) model developed by the Supply Chain Council [Supply Chain Council 2003]. The SCOR model divides a company's management processes into five central divisions (see Fig. 33):

- *Planning Processes* for the coordination of supply and demand and development of strategies, which optimally support purchase, production, and sales requirements
- *Source Processes* for purchasing the necessary quantities of goods and services
- *Make Processes* for the production of final products in their demanded quantities
- *Deliver Processes* for the preparation of final products in their demanded quantities, typically invoice completion, logistics, and distribution processes
- *Return Processes* for the cancellation of orders and product returns, which reach into the management of after sales services

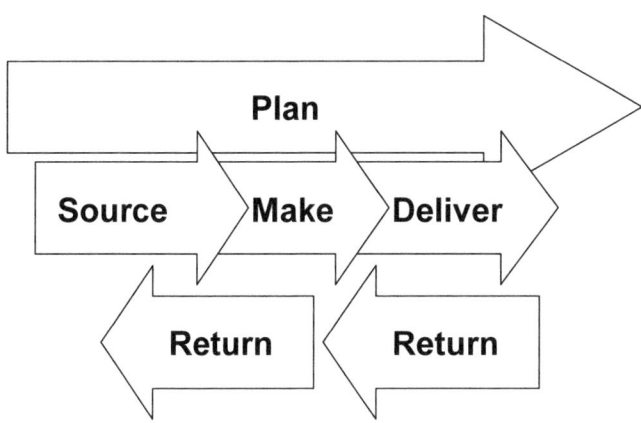

Fig. 33. SCOR model management processes

Process configurations and elements are defined for each of the five processes within the SCOR model. Through these definitions the SCOR model creates a reference process concept. This reference concept facilitates an effective interaction within a supply chain, which can be used in describing, measuring, and evaluating concrete supply chain configurations.

Complete Model of Integrated Information Management

IT service providers and customers are two elements in the supply chain of IT service production. For this reason the SCOR model's fundamental management processes are also appropriate for the design and organization of integrated information management. Fig. 34 presents an overview of the complete IIM model.

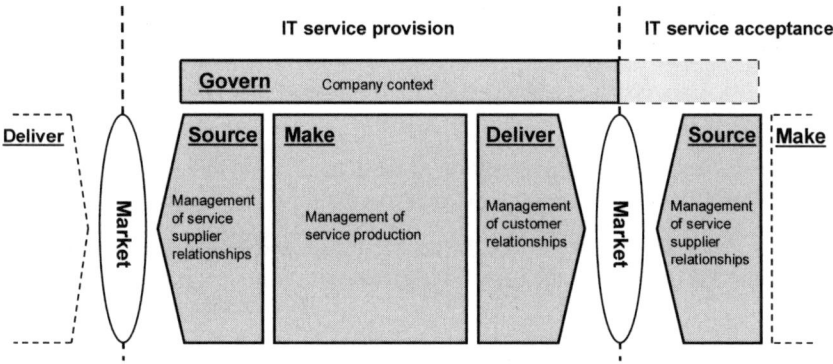

Fig. 34. Complete integrated information management (IIM) model

The tasks brought on by IT service provision and IT service acceptance (or turnover) make up the core of the model. Customers buy IT services packaged as IT service provider products. Between the two there exists a customer–supplier relationship, which is situated in a market setting. Customers are typically company business units, and an IT service provider furnishes services. If the service provider and customer find themselves within the same company or group, then an internal company market exists between them. In the case of external service providers, the market is external.

The customers' *Source Process* includes all tasks necessary for managing service suppliers' relations. It is the interface to the service provider. The IT products bought by customers flow into the *Make Processes* of the customer, either in the form of assisting business processes or a direct employment in business products.

The *service provider's Deliver Process* covers tasks necessary for the management of customer relationships. It forms the interface between the actual service production, which takes place in the context of the Make Process, and the customer's Source Process.

In the *service provider's Make Process* all tasks dedicated to the management of the IT service production are combined: the core is therefore Portfolio Management, development management, and production management. Of crucial importance here is an integrated view of service production. Although today it is common to intentionally separate IT service production into tasks of planning, development, and production, in the Make Process an output oriented, holistic view must be taken.

The service provider also has suppliers, from whom they buy products and services. These business associates can be thought of as, for example, hardware, software, or technology suppliers. The *service provider's Source Process* takes over supplier relationship management and covers all necessary, related tasks.

The supply and service chain can be continued on both sides. It is thus conceivable that customers sell their products to other customers, and likewise the supplier chain be reiterated over multiple phases.

The *Govern Process* is responsible for executive supervisory functions, organizational structures, and processes. If service providers and customers are both within the same company, then overseeing governance can exist that both sides consider authoritative. For example, governance regulations within a company can define the rules of cooperation between the service provider and customers, such that they are compulsory. External service providers, which present themselves independently on the market, usually have their own governance.

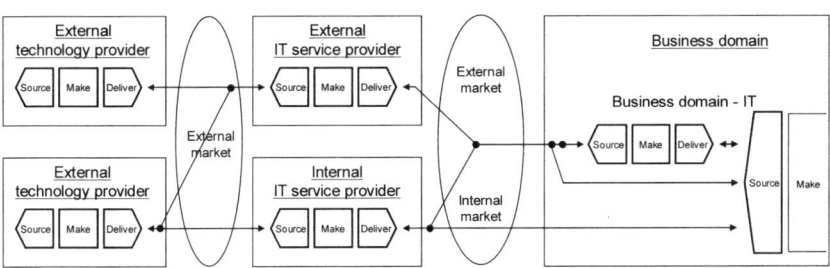

Fig. 35. Exemplifying supply and service chains for IT services

Complex supply and service chains can be orchestrated on the basis of fundamental Source–Make–Deliver mechanisms. For example, practically speaking, a 1:1 relationship does not always exist between service providers and customers. More often customers buy their IT products from different internal and external service providers. They can provide for a part of their IT services (e.g. planning or development achievements) with their own IT resources. In this way complex relational networks develop in practical business environments, as illustrated and exemplified in Fig. 35.

The actual tasks of the three core processes, namely Source, Make, and Deliver, can be structured in three levels of activity:

- At the *level of basic framework conditions*, the task focus is on the definition of fundamental, strategic specifications with respect to the processes Source, Make, and Deliver.

- The *level of the objectives* covers tasks which define tangible goals within the limits of the previously defined basic conditions.

- The *implementation level* involves tasks for controlling and actually managing the operational realization.

An overview of the real tasks within integrated information management with respect to this three level description is presented in Fig. 36.

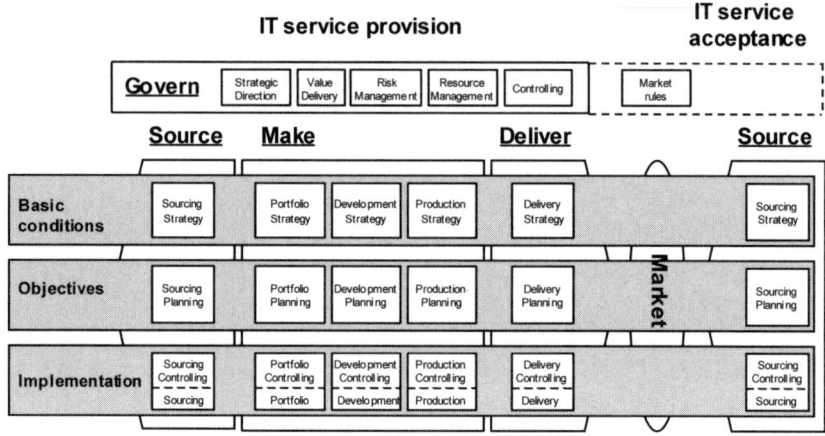

Fig. 36. Tasks within integrated information management (IIM)

3.2 Model Components

3.2.1 Govern

The term IT governance encompasses all of the principles, procedures, and measures which guarantee that allocated IT services contribute to business goal achievement and that IT resources are responsibly employed and risks appropriately supervised. Thus IT governance tasks are tasks which, from a business organizational point of view, must be managed by IT service providers. IT strategy support and even advancement of aggregate company strategy should be ensured through the establishment of leadership cycles, organizational structures, and processes.

IT governance cannot be thought of in an isolated manner, but rather as an integral component of corporate governance.

In the context of service provider and customer collaboration within a single company, IT governance has a unique significance. In this case governance defines the role of the parties involved, i.e. business units, internal IT service providers, and the CIO organization. Additionally, it must ensure that the internal market between service providers and customers operates as fluently as possible, by specifying the basic conditions and rules of the market.

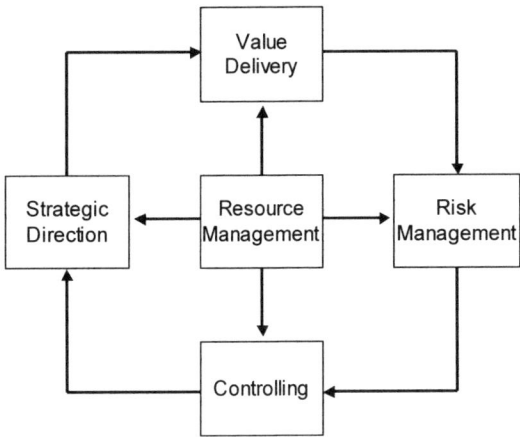

Fig. 37. IT Governance regulatory tasks [IT Governance Institute 2003]

The core tasks of IT governance can be divided into areas as illustrated in Fig. 37. These form a continuous cycle. The starting point is strategic direction, which flows into IT strategy. The implementation follows the strategy definition. During this implementation the value of the IT service provider's contribution is measured, and risks are identified and steered accordingly. Controlling supervises strategy success and directs its progression. Resources are utilized in all of the five areas. In the following descriptions, the five areas of IT governance and their allocated tasks are considered more closely:

- *IT service provider Strategic Direction*: The Strategic Direction, frequently called alignment, specifies what is required long-term from the IT service provider and its role. The origin of these details lies in the overall company strategy. The strategic business targets must reflect the service provider direction, and the organizational structure of IT must fit into the company structure. For example, if IT products are regarded within the company as commodities, then the service provider strategy must primarily be in line with a cost-efficient production of products. If, however, IT products are considered necessary for strategic competition advantages, the attention must be directed toward the service provider's capabilities and the strategic significance of future technological developments. Service provider flexibility and speed prerequisites are also determined by the overall company strategy.

  Flexibility in the sense of a flexible organizational support of customers is a central strategic objective. It can be realized by a consistent implementation of the Source–Make–Deliver principle.

  The strategic direction is fixed in the form of an IT strategy. This also includes, in addition to the service provider's fundamental roles and tasks, the definition of future core areas of business and activity.

- *Value Delivery*: The contribution of IT economic efficiency is the result of the relationship between costs and benefits. Therefore, both dimensions must be addressed in the context of IT governance. While the costs of IT utilization can usually be verified within a company relatively easily and precisely, the verification of benefit is more difficult. The IT benefit presents itself during business processes and thus is a process benefit. It is very difficult to quantify these benefits, for example, customer satisfaction, competition advantages, or employee productivity. Thus it is all the more important that the benefit of IT products is communicated in the company and is made visible, so that the discussion is not limited to cost aspects alone. This is a task belonging to IT governance. IT benefit measuring targets and objective systems should be compiled not by the service provider alone, but instead together with the business units, and consensus should be found.

  In the context of an integrated information management, the economic perspective is based on a life cycle oriented costing and performance accounting.

High economic efficiency of IT service production can be only achieved if the service provider has certain capabilities, for example: the ability to assess comprehensive and timely customer information, to have market and process effective procedures and instruments (e.g. knowledge management, power measurement), and to integrate new technologies [IT Governance Institute 2003]. The IT governance must create fitting basic conditions, so that these capabilities can be sustained and improved upon.

- *Risk Management*: Risk Management is a central element of the corporate governance, not least due to new legal requirements (e.g. the Sarbanes Oxley Act). In addition to financial risks, operational and system-dependent risks, in particular, play an ever-increasing role in this venue. These risks are in turn strongly affected by technological and data security risks. Building up from a company's general risk situation, IT-based risks must be identified, evaluated, and made transparent in the context of IT governance. Based on this information, practical strategies must then be developed to deal with these risks. A proposed strategy can consist, for example, of installing control mechanisms to minimize risks, to divide risks among partners, to insure risks, or to consciously accept them. However, even in the last case a risk analysis is essential because competent management decisions are only possible when risks are known.

A high level of transparency, which enables an early identification of risks, is possible through an integrated perspective of IT service production together with closely fitted management processes within the areas Source, Make, and Deliver.

Risk Management must not be seen as only a cost factor. Rather competitive advantages and efficiency gains can be made with its assistance, through a consistent implementation.

- *Controlling*: Goals, resources, and processes must be continuously supervised and steered to determine the service provider's level of efficiency and to promptly identify problems. It is the task of governance to identify suitable measurements and/or key indicators and to establish a steering and controlling cycle.

The IT service provider's key controlling instrument is an efficient process cost accounting.

Controlling should not focus exclusively on the financial key indicators, but should also consider, for example, using Balanced Scorecards and customer, process, and potential oriented key indicators [Boeh and Meyer 2004]. The fundamental components of the Balanced Scorecard can be adapted for use in IT, for example by aligning key indicators to the four dimensions of IT contribution to the company, IT customer orientation, future IT capabilities, and IT operational efficiency [IT Governance Institute 2003].

- *Resource Management*: The prerequisite for an IT service provider's successful implementation is an optimal employment and allocation of IT resources. These resources include both employees and IT infrastructure components, such as hardware, software, networks, or data. IT governance must define basic conditions for Resource Management within the real core processes (Source, Make, Deliver).

Resource Management must not be limited to the management and prioritization of development resources. Rather, all IT service provider resources must to be considered.

In the context of Resource Management, fundamental regulations must be set as to where and how external resources are bought, under which basic conditions new employees are hired and how employees are trained and educated, and how to establish a life cycle oriented management of hardware and software resources. Resource Management is thus always in a state of conflict. Resource Management must cope with trying to work with the most cost efficient resources and at the same time achieve as high an effectiveness of IT services as possible.

It is a precondition for a working relationship between service provider and customers to define the leeway of market participants, i.e. the rules of the market. External and internal markets must be differentiated. While the basic conditions of an external market are defined by general legal rules, IT governance defines the organization of an internal company market. The fundamental rules to define for an internal market can be divided into two categories:

- *Competition related regulations* define the rules for competition between service providers and service customers. Thereby of central importance are rules for regulating customer obligations and for the possibility of a service provider's external offering. The customer obligation specifies whether a customer is obligated to buy its IT products from a certain, usually internal company service provider or whether it may also select an external third party as provider. From an individual service customer standpoint this permission allows for external service provider contracting, which usually leads to a better competitive position and more negotiating power with the internal service provider. From a whole company perspective, capacity utilization and the service provider's economic efficiency must be taken into consideration. With this in mind an obligatory regulation for service customers to use internal service providers may be an economically sound solution.

  The same applies from a service provider's perspective. The preference of internal service providers is usually to allow for the possibility of offering products to third parties on the open market. However, as before, the question arises from a whole company perspective, whether or not the service provider can have sustainable success on a competitive external market or whether its resources would be better used in covering the needs of the internal company customers. What also play a role here are the business objectives of the service provider. If the service provider is structured as an independent profit center with an objective to turn in profits, then it must strive to sell its products to the market under optimal conditions from its perspective, alone. If, in contrast, the service provider is structured as a company internal cost center without profit objective, its primary task is to cover internal company demand for IT products.

- *Formal regulations* shape the formal relationship between service providers and service customers. Considered here, above all, are the legal relationships and service accounting mechanisms. In the context of legal relationships it must be defined, for example, how possession rights of application systems and IT infrastructures are structured. If a customer buys an IT product in the sense of a process support service, then usually the service provider remains in possession of the necessary production infrastructure, on which the product runs. It is also conceivable that the customer possesses parts of the infrastructure or holds rights to developed software. The goal of regulations for service accounting is to create as high a transparency of resulting costs and provided services as possible, but also to create incentives for sound economic behavior for both parties. A typical example is the regulation on how both sides profit from technical progress. Usually rapid technological progress allows internal IT service providers to manufacture products at continuously lower prices. If the internal service provider does not pass this progress on to its customers, then an efficient IT utilization for customers is not possible. If this increase in efficiency is totally passed on to customers, no incentive exists for service providers to reach for technological progress. The market regulations must be formulated so that for both sides an economically sound interaction is possible.

3.2.2 Source

The Source Process is the link between the service provider's Deliver Process and the customer's Make Process. In IT the term sourcing is usually thought of in connection with the discussion around in- or outsourcing. However in the IIM model, it covers all tasks with regard to the management of suppliers' relationships. Positioned in the middle are those tasks which are necessary for purchasing required IT products.

The design and arrangement of a purchase process strongly depends on the kind of products purchased. Therefore, the special properties of IT products are emphasized here again:

- IT products are not capital goods, but services, which are used by customers continuously, over a longer period.
- IT products are subject to frequent changes, i.e. they develop continuously.
- Users call upon IT products while executing business processes. The IT product execution time cannot be planned in detail beforehand.
- A large number of each IT product is usually needed.

Sourcing can take place at both the IT service provider's and IT service customer's location.

However, the service provider's Source Process differs from that of the customer not only in the kind of IT products purchased. Thus in the following section the two Source Processes within the IIM model are briefly described.

The IT Service Provider's Source Process

The service provider's Source Process corresponds to the classical concept of outsourcing. It covers those tasks which are necessary to manage outsourcing relationships with service providers. Fig. 38 illustrates this fundamental concept with an example of an IT service provider, which acts as a service provider for the business units. Those IT services which are not provided by the service provider itself (internal contribution) will be bought from external technology suppliers in the sense of an outsourcing purchase (external supply). The proportion of products provided by internal contribution (manufacturing depth) of the IT service provider and the decision as to which concrete services will be bought-in are strategic decisions and must be defined in the Sourcing Strategy.

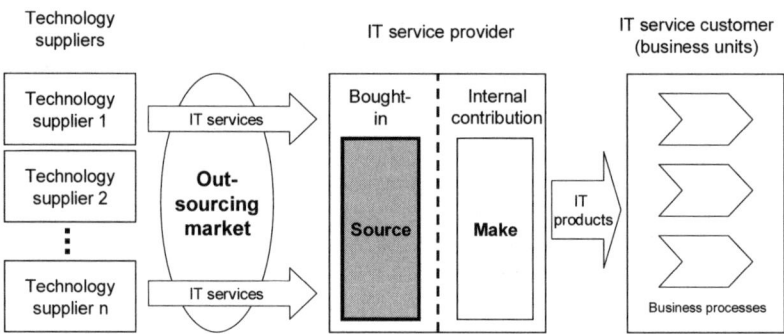

Fig. 38. IT service provider's Source Process

In practice the following IT services are typically bought-in from the outsourcing market:

- Purchase of hardware resources (e.g. computing power, memory, etc. in the context of an outsourcing of computer center operations)

- Purchase of personnel resources (e.g. external development resources in low-wage countries)·

- Purchase of software solutions (e.g. in the context of application service providing)
- Purchase of hardware components (e.g. computer systems, printers, etc.)

The purchased IT services flow into the IT products sold by the service provider to the customer. The higher the percentage of bought-in IT services is to all IT services offered, the more the service provider is acting as a pure service integrator.

IT Customer's Source Processes

The concept of Source Processes for IT products has not yet become common practice with customers. Above all, this is because in the past IT cooperation between customers and service providers was strongly project-driven. The fundamental idea that customers should fulfill their IT requirements in the form of IT product purchases is only gradually gaining acceptance. Fig. 39 illustrates this fundamental interaction. A company's business units buy their required IT products from one or more internal or external service providers.

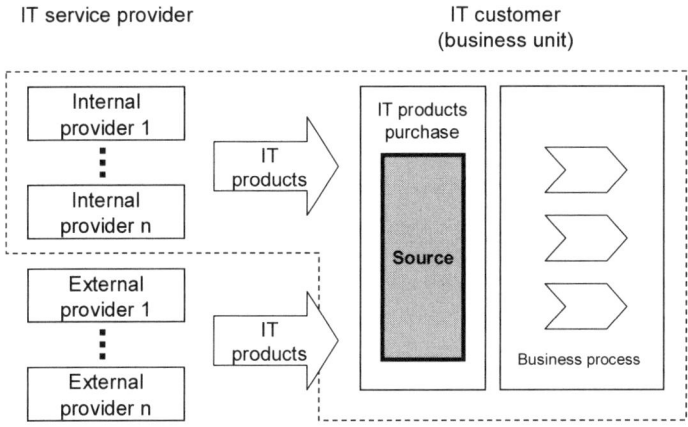

Fig. 39. Source Process using the IT customer as an example

An IT customer's Source Process is necessarily and markedly dynamic, due to the unique properties of IT products, in particular the frequent changes they undergo.

> *Portfolio Management takes on a central role in the organization of the customer–supplier relationship between service providers and service customers.*

Portfolio Management must recognize how dynamic IT sourcing is. In order to handle this dynamic, IT products must be packaged so as to fulfill customer requirements, and at the same time service production must be economically efficient (see Chapter 2.1, Fig. 4). A product portfolio, which meets market demand, can only be achieved through a holistic approach to Portfolio Management. Such an approach also minimizes the probability of incompatibilities between IT products.

Customer Source Processes are especially effective when premium, business process oriented IT products are bought. Examples of these products are:

- Purchasing an email service
- Purchasing an IT workstation service
- Purchasing a personnel process (e.g. wage and salary statement production), including the interface to financial accounting
- Purchasing an electronic selling process (e.g. electronic ticket production)
- Purchasing IT services providing ISDN connections

Independent of where a sourcing takes place, either at the service provider's or service customer's location, there are several tasks to be tackled in the context of the Source Process. These tasks are defined at three levels within the IIM model, Sourcing Strategy, Sourcing Planning, and Sourcing Controlling (see Fig. 40). Here they will be described in greater detail.

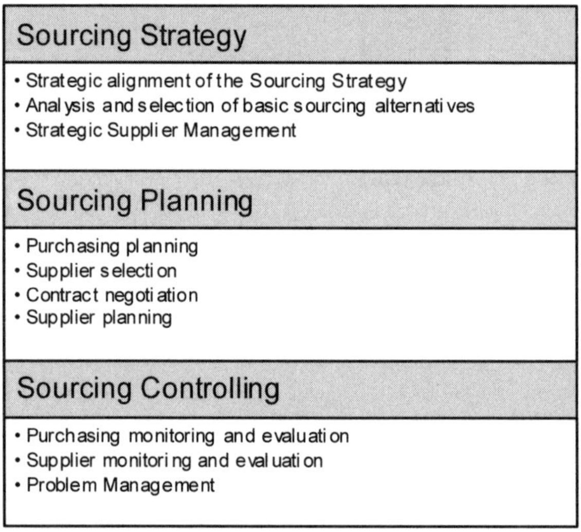

Sourcing Strategy
- Strategic alignment of the Sourcing Strategy
- Analysis and selection of basic sourcing alternatives
- Strategic Supplier Management

Sourcing Planning
- Purchasing planning
- Supplier selection
- Contract negotiation
- Supplier planning

Sourcing Controlling
- Purchasing monitoring and evaluation
- Supplier monitoring and evaluation
- Problem Management

Fig. 40. Tasks with Source Processes

3.2.2.1 Sourcing Strategy

In the Sourcing strategy the fundamental long-term conditions are specified for the Source Process. The guidelines and objectives for Sourcing Planning and Sourcing Controlling are defined. The strategy can be held in a sourcing governance model, which is a part of the overall IT governance model. The following tasks are assigned to the strategic level:

- *Strategic alignment of the Sourcing Strategy*: A Sourcing Strategy is not made for and by itself, but should contribute to a company's pursuit of its business goals. It is with this in mind that the Sourcing Strategy must be coordinated with company strategy and support, for example, business goals regarding flexibility, innovation, costs, or quality.

    Not only IT service providers or CIO organizations, but business units as service customers must also define IT Sourcing Strategies.

    The starting point is always the understanding of IT products as services supporting business processes. Goals of Sourcing Strategies can be, for example, reacting as quickly as possible to changes in qualitative and quantitative demand of IT products, creating cost advantages, or having access to innovative IT products. The decision on the role of IT within a company has a significant influence on the Sourcing Strategy. Should IT products be very valuable within a company's core processes, this usually leads to IT service production being regarded as a core business competence. These IT products then support and represent direct competitive advantages or innovative business products. In this case, a high degree of internal IT product manufacturing and a comprehensive internal IT expertise are strategic alternatives. If, however, IT products are regarded as commodities, then purchasing external service providers' products is of substantially greater importance.

    Furthermore, a service customer can decide in the context of its IT strategy for different degrees of IT support for its business processes and business products. So it is conceivable, for example, that one service customer requests a high level of IT support for its selling process, while another requires only a minimum of IT service support for its selling process. This decision has a great influence on the service customer's IT demanded portfolio. That means, in the context of the Source Process, the kind and scope of IT products which are to be purchased.

- *Analysis and selection of fundamental sourcing alternatives*: Depending on a company's business and IT strategies, obtainable sourcing alternatives must be analyzed and selected in the context of Sourcing Strategy. Sourcing alternatives can be categorized along different dimensions [Jouanne-Diedrich 2004]. Alternatives can be differentiated, for example, as a function of the number of desired supplier relationships, i.e. between single sourcing and multi-sourcing. Regarding the degree of external procurement, the alternatives total outsourcing, selective outsourcing (also known as Smart Sourcing), or total insourcing are to be considered. The location of potential service providers can also be pursued in this Sourcing Strategy. Here the choice is between a Nearshore Sourcing Strategy and an Offshore Sourcing Strategy (also known as Global Sourcing).

- *Strategic Supplier Management*: The goal of Strategic Supplier Management is to establish long-term partnerships and objectives with service providers. The market for IT service providers is in a state of constant change and therefore defines the framework within which Supplier Management must make its strategic decisions.

Most importantly, an IT service provider must be capable of delivering reliable products over a longer period of time and be flexible enough to realize change requests efficiently and effectively for its customers.

There are other variables in the Sourcing Strategy equation. Service provider efficiency and offering change and trends develop (e.g. increasing globalization and networking). A good example for this is the growing market of service providers, who offer Business Process Outsourcing (BPO). With the increasing maturity of the BPO market, service customers are presented with new possibilities for organizing their Sourcing Strategies, which go further than classic approaches (those regarding infrastructure sourcing). The ground rules of cooperation with service providers are to be defined in the context of strategic supplier management. These ground rules include the strategic objectives of the partnership, with respect to services, costs, and quality. Additionally, the fundamental principles of the supply and service relationship must be agreed upon, such as the legal framework, the distribution of risks, or the escalation and conciliation processes.

For the organization of strategic supplier management, existing concepts and instruments from strategic purchasing can be implemented for strategic IT sourcing, for example, concepts such as Supplier Relationship Management (SRM).

3.2.2.2 Sourcing Planning

Sourcing Planning defines, under the basic conditions given by the Sourcing Strategy, the concrete objectives of the Source Process. The following planning tasks are thus to be performed:

- *Purchase Planning*: The goal of Purchase Planning is to specify the required IT products so that negotiations with potential IT service providers can be initiated. Purchase planning usually receives the necessary information in the form of a performance specification, which was compiled within the Make and Deliver Processes and defines which functionalities the single or multiple IT products must cover, what the quality requirements are, and what quantities of information are to be dealt with. When dealing with complex IT products, it may be advantageous to include potential service providers in purchase planning.

- *Supplier selection*: In a second step, based on the concrete product specification defined in purchase planning, all potential service providers must be evaluated and the best provider selected. Again, as in strategic supplier management, the long-term strength and consistency of a supplier plays a special role. For the selection process, selection criteria can be defined and supplemented by Best Practice information. Important selection criteria are, for example, service provider's process, technology, and industry expertise, reference customers and projects, flexibility during contract design, the experience and availability of human resources, and company culture [Stone 2002a].

- *Contract negotiation*: If a service provider is selected, then in the context of Sourcing Planning negotiations begin, which result in a contract. As in SLAs, the contract defines the basic conditions for executing IT products, the quality characteristics of IT products, and the realization of new requirements and/or product alternatives.

- *Supplier Planning*: Strategic Supplier Management defines the long-term basic conditions for cooperation with individual IT service providers. Based on this and within the context of Supplier Planning, an agreement is made on mid-term objectives. With these agreements, for example, annual quality and cost goals can be defined with each individual service provider.

3.2.2.3 Sourcing Controlling

The operational realization of the Source Process takes place in the context of Sourcing Controlling. This typically covers the following tasks:

- *Purchase monitoring and evaluation*: The promises made while purchasing the IT products take center stage in the monitoring of costs and quality. Activities such as monitoring service provider billing accounts or monitoring product due date delivery come to mind here. The service monitoring is based upon the negotiated and accepted SLAs. In the context of Sourcing Controlling, service provider promises, documented in SLAs, are to be supervised continuously to ensure that they are indeed kept.

- *Supplier monitoring and evaluation*: Not only the delivered IT products, but also the service provider, itself, should be supervised and evaluated. For example, it should be regularly evaluated whether the objectives agreed upon during supplier planning are kept, whether the quality of the service provider is in line with expectations, and whether the service provider relationship is developing positively. For this purpose conventional concepts from purchasing can be used, such as SRM, also for controlling the IT service provider.

- *Problem Management*: If, in the context of the various tasks of monitoring, problems or deviations are identified, then it is task of Sourcing Controlling to solve these anomalies together with the service provider. If this is not possible, then escalation and conciliation mechanisms defined in Sourcing Strategy are to be introduced.

The previously described tasks also appear in other IT sourcing concepts. Example 7 describes such a concept, the Sourcing Life Cycle by Gartner Research.

The question of interest here is how the organizational implementation of the Source Process should take place. Fig. 41 presents a possible role model, within which this task is taken on by the CIO organization. The CIO organization is then the interface between the operational business units and the IT service providers. A Sourcing Office is responsible for general sourcing tasks.

Sourcing Managers, in a sense like buyers, take on the interface function between the service provider's Product Managers and the business unit's process owner for one or more IT products.

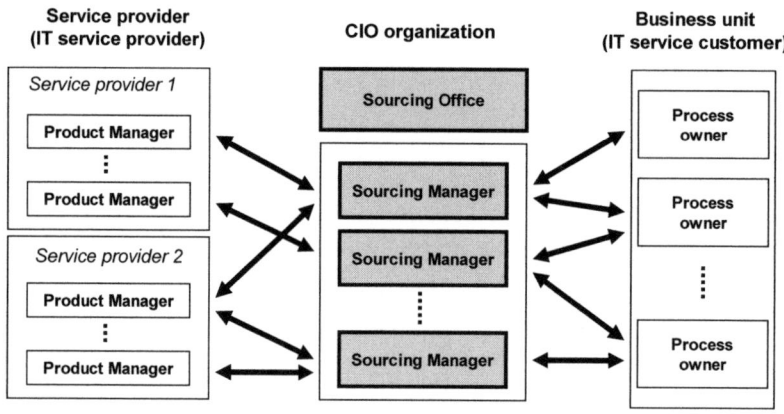

Fig. 41. Rolls within the Source Process

The *Sourcing Office* is responsible, in particular, for the following tasks:
- Definition of the Sourcing Strategy
- Analysis and selection of the service provider
- Contract negotiations and design of SLAs
- Evaluation of service providers

Ex. 7. Sourcing Life Cycle by Gartner Research [Stone 2002b]

Gartner Research divides the life cycle of outsourcing relationships into four phases as presented in Fig. 42. These correspond more or less to the three levels of tasks in the Source Process of the IIM model. Phase 1 corresponds to the Sourcing Strategy, phases 2 and 3 to Sourcing Planning, and phase 4 to Sourcing Controlling.

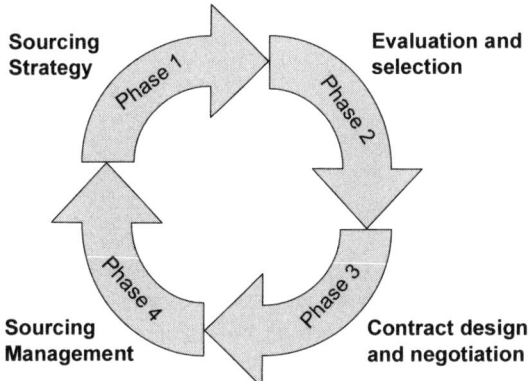

Fig. 42. Sourcing Life Cycle by Gartner Research

According to Gartner Research the four phases are defined as follows:

Sourcing Strategy: The definition of a comprehensive Sourcing Strategy, at the heart of which is coordination of business and IT strategy, and in which the current and desired states are precisely described.

Evaluation and selection: The implementation of a structured evaluation process, with which the best service provider for a given task can be identified.

Contract design and negotiation: A durable developmental process for contracts, which are acceptable for both contracting parties on a longer time horizon.

Sourcing Management: A strong governance model for the outsourcing relationship, which can be easily adapted to a modification of basic conditions.

The central tasks and success factors are described for each phase.

A Sourcing Manager takes on the active management of interfaces between service providers and the real service customers. He is the main customer contact for the service provider. Alternatively, for the process owner, the Sourcing Manager is again the main contact for all questions and tasks with regard to procuring necessary IT products. With regard to interface management the Product Manager is responsible for the following tasks:

- IT product planning together with process owners
- IT product procurement and IT product monitoring
- Costing and scheduling monitoring
- Service provider monitoring
- Problem management
- Monitoring and evaluation

3.2.3 Deliver

The Deliver Process is the interface between the service provider and the service customer. Contrary to a limited definition of Delivery, which in IT usually focuses primarily on the provision of IT services, within integrated information management the Deliver Process covers all tasks necessary for organizing relationships between service providers and their IT product sales market, i.e. their service customers. These tasks include, first of all, the dynamic positioning of the product offering on the market and the design of the marketing mix.

> *The most important task of the Deliver Process is it to transform the IT customer's requests into internal requirement specifications for IT service production.*

The Deliver Process has an additional function as a mediator between the service provider's Make Process, within which IT services required for IT products are designed and manufactured, and the service customer's Source Process, which is responsible for procuring IT products (see Fig. 43). The interface to service customers is built upon business perspectives; however, the internal interface to the Make Process takes on a more technical view. The significant benefit of the Deliver Process comes from transforming the customer and market requirements from a business view into a technical view of IT service production, and vice versa.

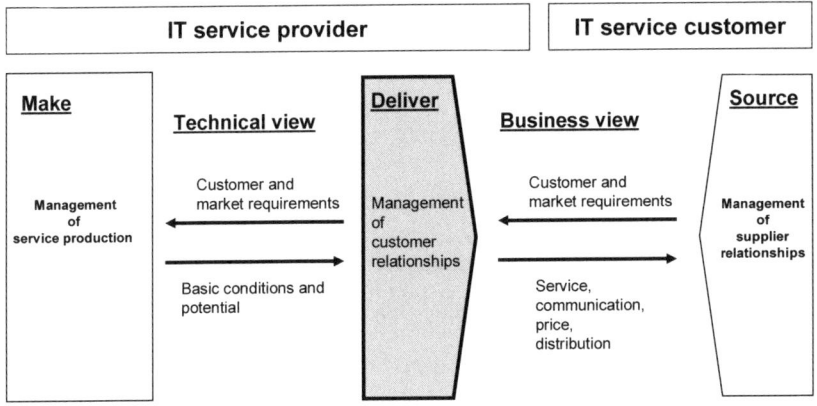

Fig. 43. Mediating function of the Deliver Process between service provider and customer

In the context of the Deliver Process, customer and market requirements must be identified. Based on these requirements, the offering to be made to customers and internal service production must be designed and organized. It is within the Deliver Process that the real product market offering is designed, and customer and market requirements are promptly and comprehensively communicated to internal service production.

The relationship between service providers and service customers is based on pure business considerations. Service customers have no influence on the technical design of the IT services necessary for an IT product.

The Deliver Process receives information from the Make Process about internal basic conditions and where potential lies in IT service production, which is important for designing product offers to customers. This includes, for example, information about development capacities, production capacities, current performance program, and future technological developments.

In the following, the Deliver Process' central tasks are described, divided into three elements, namely, Delivery Strategy, Delivery Planning, and Delivery Controlling, (see Fig. 44).

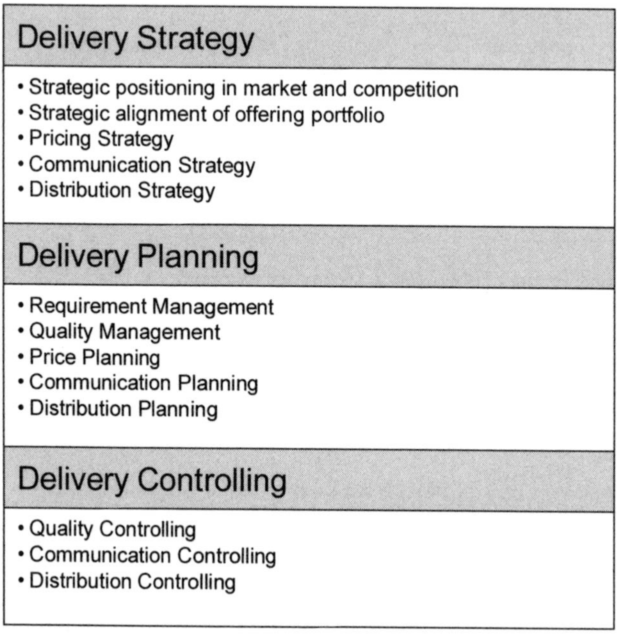

Delivery Strategy
• Strategic positioning in market and competition • Strategic alignment of offering portfolio • Pricing Strategy • Communication Strategy • Distribution Strategy
Delivery Planning
• Requirement Management • Quality Management • Price Planning • Communication Planning • Distribution Planning
Delivery Controlling
• Quality Controlling • Communication Controlling • Distribution Controlling

Fig. 44. Deliver Process tasks

3.2.3.1 *Delivery Strategy*

The Delivery Strategy defines the IT service provider's position in the market and competitive ranking, and ensures that the direction of its product program moves with market trends. In this context, whether the market is internal and guided by governance regulations or external and defined by competitors is actually is of no consequence. Another goal here is the formation and preservation of long-term, stable relations with service customers. Within the Delivery Strategy the following tasks must be carried out:

- *Strategic positioning in the market and competitive ranking*: Here, the bylaws of the service provider's relevant market, customer, and competition segments stand in the foreground. Under these bylaws, the business environment must be analyzed with regard to markets, customers, and competitors. A number of established methods are available for the business environment analysis. These include scenario analyses, competition analyses, benchmarking, SWOT analyses, portfolio techniques, Balanced Scorecards, Early Detection, or market research. All of these instruments are available to support the positioning of the service provider.

- *Strategic alignment of the offering portfolio*: The service provider's offering portfolio should be in line with customer demand as much as possible. To reach this end, already at the strategic level, customer long-term expectations of products, especially with regard to quality, costs, and price must be identified and taken into consideration. The starting point is, of course, customer requirements and the thus derived concrete customer benefit. It is therefore a task within Delivery Strategy to present Performance Planning and Development (which takes place within the Make Process) with information about external markets and customer needs.

  The service provider must have a product catalog and lucid understanding of the effect of its IT products on the service customers' processes.

  Furthermore, customer needs must be identified and acknowledged promptly with regard to product innovations, product variations, and product discontinuation. Taking the Internet service provider as an example, it must seek out customer needs for its product "Internet Access." The service provider must evaluate customer demand for product innovations (e.g. free access services or flat rate offers), for product variations (e.g. different bandwidths or monthly transmission quantities), or product discontinuation (e.g. due to unattractive prices). Such needs should result in modifications of marketing strategy and in new products.

- *Pricing Strategy*: Questions dealing with price positioning, price distinction, pricing logic, and price bundling are to be addressed in accordance with the overall IT strategy [Sebastian and Maessen 2003]. For example, the definition of a service provider's strategic price positioning can result in a position of high or low price competitor. If business units tend toward internally manufacturing IT services, then the Pricing Strategy also takes on the job of strategic controlling of the Make or Buy decision. With a choice of strategy, market aspects must be considered (i.e. is the target market segment suitable for a low price strategy?) and internal aspects (i.e. is it possible to be a low-price bidder and thus necessarily cost leader under the current production costs and conditions?). In the context of a strategy of price distinction, the question arises at to how much the evaluation of different payment schedules of individual customer segments can be used in designing individual customer prices. The pricing logic determines base prices, pricing progressions, the number of price alternatives, and the pricing procedure. The pricing procedure plays a special role in the relationship of the service provider with its internal customers. Price bundling strategies combine several products together, which are offered at a package price. This can serve not only to reduce customer price transparency and price sensitivity, but also to induce customers to pay a higher sum price. An internal company IT service provider must be able to justify its Pricing Strategy in the context of IT governance.

- *Communication Strategy*: The Communication Strategy establishes the service provider's communication goals and target groups. It chooses the fundamental communication instruments with respect to advertising, sales promotion and public work.

The service customer is informed through an active communication strategy about the service provider's objectives and efficiency.

The internal IT service provider must also manage an active marketing. The resulting costs for this are often questioned internally, because customers fear that by way of an internal marketing, the internal service provider's poor quality IT products are put in a better light.

An internal marketing promotes communication between the service provider and its customers. The benefits of internal marketing must be actively communicated to both parties. These benefits are most apparent in a better mutual planning and coordination.

- *Distribution Strategy*: Here in the Distribution Strategy the basic conditions are decided upon as to how and through what channels products are available to customers. For external IT service providers the sales strategy lies at the heart of the distribution strategy. The sales strategy specifies which sales models are to be implemented (e.g. single-step or multi-level sales) and which sales forms are to be selected (e.g. selective or exclusive selling). Furthermore, it defines how sales partners must be supported, for example, through push or pull activities.

The kind of marketed products has a great influence on the Distribution Strategy, in particular on logistics. IT products usually consist not only of physical components, but also intangible components, which can be distributed electronically. However, their respective proportions of the total product vary greatly. Thus the IT product Desktop Service consists of many physical elements, for example the installation of a PC at a workplace, the cabling of network connections, the delivery of printers, and on-site support. In contrast, an IT product Internet-based Online Timetable Information requires, if at all, very few decentralized physical elements, which must be made available by the service provider.

The Distribution Strategy includes also developing strategies for service bases and subsidiaries, for the transportation and delivery of the physical product components and for cooperation scenarios with selling partners.

3.2.3.2 Delivery Planning

The fundamental basic conditions defined in Delivery Strategy must be concretely itemized in Delivery Planning and augmented with objectives. Delivery Planning should thus cover the following tasks:

- *Requirement Management*: The service provider's product portfolio must be aligned to customer requirements.

The exact identification and specification of customer requirements is a prerequisite for IT product design, and therefore is the foundation of an effective Portfolio Management.

Usually the specification is given the form of a requirement analysis. Although today this task, in practice, is usually given to IT development units, within integrated information management it is a central element of Delivery Planning. Only through this assignment, can it be guaranteed that service providers have a uniform, business oriented perspective of Requirement Management; that also, with regard to requirement analysis, all service production subsystems are given equal attention. IT product customer requirements change frequently in the course of the product's use.

The Requirement Management for IT products is a continuous, enduring activity and not a project-bound, punctual task.

- *Quality Management*: The superordinate goals of IT Quality Management are defined in the customer-specific guaranteed quality characteristic descriptions of the IT products, which are used for reporting purposes and to monitor current quality states.

Quality Management is then product-related when formulated in SLAs.

A service level defines the quality criteria of a product and, when necessary, is customer specific. Both technical quality criteria and customer-relevant quality criteria are agreed upon. Technical quality criteria can include, for example, availability ratios, response times, or capacities. Customer-relevant criteria can include cost savings, beneficial effects, or customer satisfaction. In order to be able to negotiate SLAs with existing and new customers, customers must have a comprehensive understanding of the service provider's product offering. For this reason the first core responsibility of Quality Management is to design and create an IT product catalog. Many IT service providers have trouble with this task since few empirical values are available, and thus there is great uncertainty in the precise descriptions to be put in a product catalog. This applies, for example, to the design of the catalog structure and the content type and form, which are described for each product in the catalog. The product catalog can be used as a foundation for the process of IT Quality Management. This then leads to the process being divided into three phases, which form a cycle:

Implementation of new quality criteria: In a first step the IT product quality criteria are formulated together with customers. The quality criteria are based on the customer requirements outlined in the requirement analysis. These requirements are, at the same time, a vital input to Portfolio Management during the Make Process, in which the internal planning of IT services takes place. In a second step, if an SLA draft is at hand, it is the basis of negotiations with customers and can be fixed firmly in the case of an agreement.

Management of actual product quality: All agreed upon quality criteria must be constantly monitored evaluated. This operational task is a part of Delivery Control and is described further below.

Periodic evaluation of product quality: Existing agreements and contracts must be examined and adapted regularly. In the context of monitoring, insight and evaluations gained about individual customer and contractual relations are the foundation on which examinations and adaptations are made.

- *Price Planning*: While the Pricing Strategy specifies the fundamental organizational framework of pricing politics, product and customer-specific prices are set during Price Planning. The results of Price Planning are an important input for Quality Management, especially in the drafting and negotiating phases of new SLAs. For example, in price planning for new products price calculations must be made, market prices set, and profit margins fixed. Pricing politics, e.g. price discounts, price surcharges, or supplements must also be analyzed. Prices for existing products must be regularly examined and adapted to changing prerequisite conditions of both internal and external origin. The concrete conditions for delivery, billing, and financing must be set.

  Internal IT service providers are usually given a predetermined budget, with which their scope of action is constrained. For budget planning, service customers' needs, with respect to IT products, must be identified and understood. Here, in particular, the quantity planning of service customers plays an important role, i.e. an estimation of required number per IT product.

- *Communication Planning*: Communication Planning specifies the custom specific communication instruments and plans their implementation. For example, target segments for communication measures must be specified, communication contents defined, communication events regarding start and duration fixed, resources planned, media and partners identified and selected, contract negotiations with communication partners held and confirmed in contracts. Beyond that, customer specific tasks of planning also exist; among these are, for example, the selection of customer specific communication instruments, planning of customer visits, and the measurement and evaluation of customer satisfaction.

- *Distribution Planning*: Following the Distribution Strategy precise distribution measures must be planned. Distribution channels and sales partners must be identified and contacted, negotiations with potential partners held, and sales contracts fixed. The geographical and personnel planning of service support bases and subsidiaries need to be configured and, correspondingly, concepts for logistic, storage, and transportation must be developed.

3.2.3.3 Delivery Controlling

Delivery Strategy and Planning with their goals and objectives affect the design of Delivery Controlling. Delivery Controlling is responsible for the realization of planned tasks. It steers and directs the operational delivery procedures. Among the tasks of Delivery Controlling are:

- *Quality Controlling*: The main responsibility of Quality Controlling is to continually monitor the agreed quality criteria of IT products. This applies in particular to the customer-relevant characteristics of cost, quality, and scheduling of the provided IT products. The measurements necessary for monitoring are usually set within the Make Process, and carried out in particular during production. Within Quality Controlling these measurements are evaluated and summarized in the form of consequential reports.

  Evaluations and reports must be designed for customers, i.e. business oriented and non-technical operating figures and volumes.

  Often service customers are presented with many measured technical variables, which have little meaning and thus are of little value to them. Therefore, already in the context of quality management, the reporting guidelines should be defined together with customers. These guidelines must be adhered to in Quality Controlling. If quality criteria are not met, Quality Controlling is responsible for the initiation of improvement measures, both internal and external. Furthermore, the operational tasks of Quality Controlling include accounting and invoicing of sold products.

- *Communication Controlling*: Here there is a controlling of segment and customer-specific communication instruments. The segment-specific activities include, for example, the monitoring of publicity campaigns, the measurement and evaluation of communication quality, and the reporting of success of communication measures. The customer-specific measures defined in Communication Planning (e.g. customer visits or customer events) must be measured and evaluated with respect to both cost and quality. In addition, instruments for monitoring customer behavior can be put to use here.

- *Distribution Controlling*: In Distribution Controlling planned selling and logistics concepts are to be monitored continuously. Disturbances or erroneous trends should be promptly detected and eliminated through improvement measures.

  An IT service provider must monitor and direct both the distribution of its IT products and the decentralized IT production infrastructure components.

  The distribution of IT products is to be monitored with respect to both quantity and time. The quality properties of distribution are described in the context of Quality Management of the individual IT products. For the IT business in addition to the distribution of the explicit IT products, the distribution of decentralized components of IT production infrastructure plays a significant role. Customers must have physically installed, for example, workstation systems, networks, and printers in order for IT products to be delivered at all.

3.2.4 Make

The Make Process is responsible for the management of IT service production. In the Deliver Process IT products to be sold to customers take center stage; however, in the Make Process, planning, development, and production of IT services for products is of utmost importance. The Make Process thus dominates the internal view of IT service providers.

The Make Process can be divided into three subareas, which are based on an industrial manufacturing orientation (see Ex. 8):

- Portfolio Management (management of service programs)
- Development Management (management of service organization and design)
- Production Management (management of service production)

> **Ex. 8.** Industrial service production process
>
> The process of industrial service production can be divided, as depicted in Fig. 45, into the two major tasks of program planning and order processing. The process is subject to the target goals and objectives previously described in Chapter 2.3 and implements various production resources. The core of program planning is made up of planning and controlling production and sales programs, i.e. all elements of produced services. Program planning covers strategic tasks (e.g. defining the service assortment), tactical tasks (e.g. describing individual services more precisely), and operational tasks (e.g. defining the type, quantity, and quality of produced services within a single period.
>
> The process of order processing consists of three major tasks, namely, development/construction, order preparation, and production/assembly. Thereby the actual process organization must adapt to market requirements. Thus there is a difference between, for example, the order processing of a program producer who produces standard products for bulk markets (e.g. production of Desktop Services) and the individual order producer who produces customer-specific products for special orders (e.g. production of reports from a data warehouse).
>
> It is interesting to note that until now, in practice, order preparation as a task within IT service production is only a task, if at all, with respect to purchasing big computer hosts. Order preparation builds a link between

development and production. The goal is to guarantee service production with an optimal implementation of all production processes. It is of no surprise that the absence of order preparation leads to a poor coordination of development and production in the production of IT services. The definition and realization of tasks concerning work order preparation within the process of IT service production is thus a main emphasis of integrated information management. This applies especially in the context of Production Planning and Controlling.

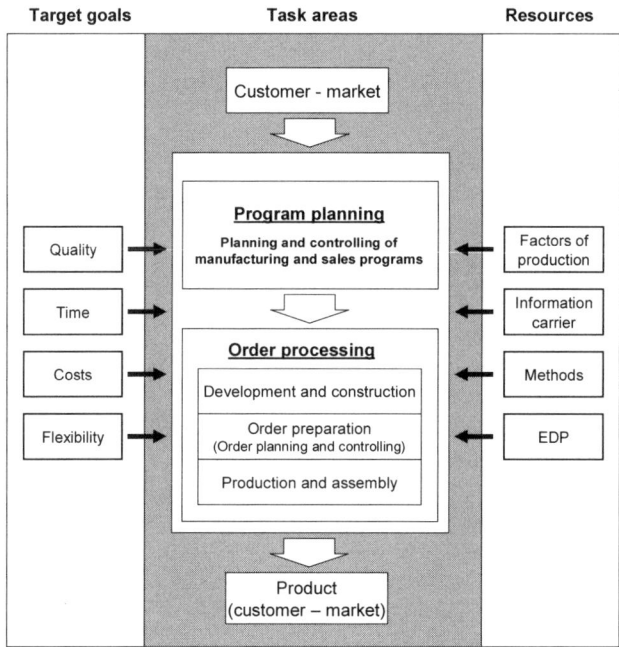

Fig. 45. Industrial process for service production (following [Eversheim 1990])

An integrated, output oriented view of the three subareas of the Make Process is of central importance. IT services are the output of the Make Process. The coordination of the three subareas is a prerequisite for these services, enabling the design of both marketable and customer-desirable products. No subarea alone can accomplish this feat. For example, from a development perspective wonderfully designed services can, by not considering production limits, lead to quality and cost production problems which are obvious to service customers. Despite outstanding development and production, a bad Portfolio Management can again lead to the production of services which are of no benefit to customers and thus cannot be sold in sufficient quantities. Such problems can only be avoided when tasks within the three subareas are coordinated with one another and holistic management processes exist. Thus in the following description of the three subareas of the Make Process, their relationships to the other processes within the IIM model will be pointed out repeatedly.

The dominant approach today, the Plan–Build–Run approach to IT service production, is once again reflected in the three subareas of the Make Process. However, partitioning the Make Process into strategic, planning, and controlling levels of activity (see Fig. 46) presents a significant difference. In business practice the Plan–Build–Run approach leads to a planning that is primarily strategic, a development that is primarily planning, and a production that is primarily operational. Fig. 46 shows that as a consequence a number of task topics in the Make Process go unaccounted for. In contrast, integrated information management emphasizes the vertical and horizontal integration of tasks.

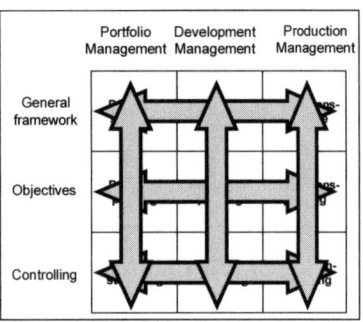

Fig. 46. Emphasis of Plan, Build, Run and Integrated Information Models

3.2.4.1 Portfolio Management

In Portfolio Management the service provider's service program offering is designed and organized. The service program is the sum of all individual services offered by the service provider. For many IT service providers the active design and creation of a service program is a new task. Questions such as "In which service segments we should be participate?", "What does our present service program look like?", "What strategy must we pursue to reach our preferred portfolio?" and "In what service segments are our services even competitive?" are quite unusual to ask (see also [Dietrich and Schirra 2004]).

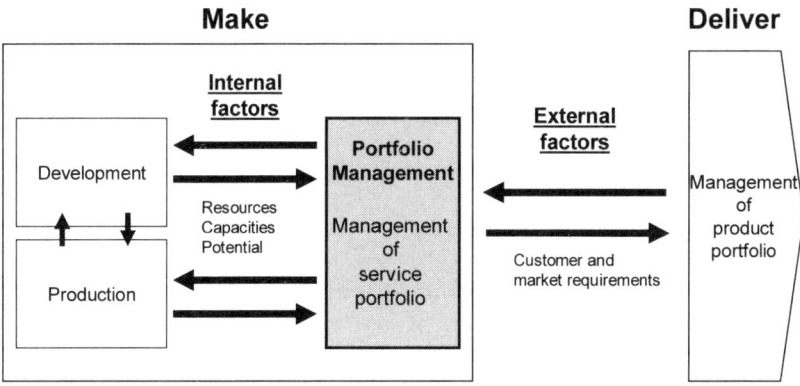

Fig. 47. Differentiation between Portfolio Management and the Deliver Process

Although Portfolio Management has a reciprocal relationship with the Deliver Process and a number of interfaces exist between both processes, it is important to emphasize the different aspects of both processes (see Fig. 47). The Deliver Process is based an external view, which is formed by market and customer requirements and constraints. Accordingly, the Deliver Process concentrates on the design and organization of sales portfolios, in which IT products are included. Of course, this external view also plays a role within Portfolio Management. However, Portfolio Management must extend even further to incorporate internal factors from development and production.

It is the mission of Portfolio Management to design, organize, and steer the service program, which is the sum of all of a service provider's IT services.

External and internal factors together form the guidelines for Portfolio Management. Information flows from the Deliver Process into Portfolio Management and vice versa.

Portfolio Management tasks can be classified, as thus far has been the case, as belonging to the strategic, planning, or controlling level (see Fig. 48).

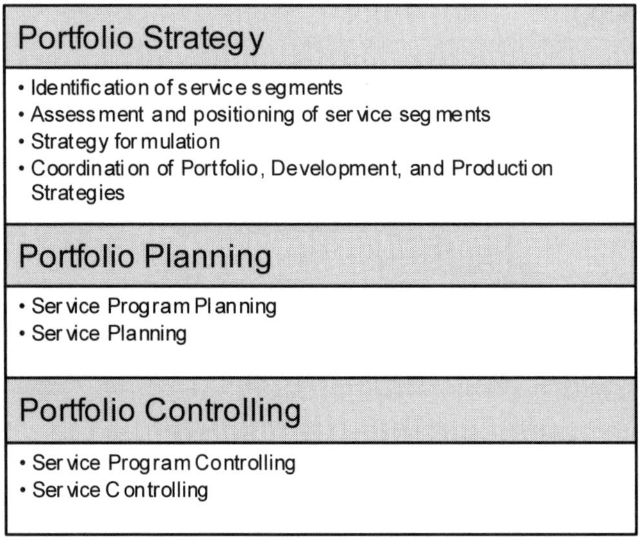

Portfolio Strategy
- Identification of service segments
- Assessment and positioning of service segments
- Strategy formulation
- Coordination of Portfolio, Development, and Production Strategies

Portfolio Planning
- Service Program Planning
- Service Planning

Portfolio Controlling
- Service Program Controlling
- Service Controlling

Fig. 48. Portfolio Management tasks

Portfolio Strategy

The Portfolio Strategy defines the strategy for the IT service provider's service portfolio. Strategy development follows the strategic planning process. It must identify high-yield sustainable service segments and define an orienting and organizational framework for Portfolio Planning and Portfolio Controlling [Schweitzer 1994]. In the sense of a planning outline, it specifies the entire range of the service provider's activities on a long-term basis. Thus, Portfolio Strategy concentrates on service segments and not on individual, real services. It covers the following tasks:

- *Identification of service segments*: The service segments to be identified are those which promise long-term market success. For this purpose information regarding both markets and customers is required from the Delivery Strategy (e.g. customer segments, market analyses, or demand forecasts). Information from the Development and Production Strategy is required as well (e.g. regarding technological innovations, new development and production procedures, or technological and organizational general frameworks).

- *Evaluation and positioning of service segments*: In a second step the identified service segments must assessed and compared with one another. Usually Portfolio Analysis methods are employed here. Service segments are assessed within a given evaluation roster and compared in what is usually a multidimensional matrix. Existing service segments can be presented in an actual portfolio and be moved together with new service segments into a target portfolio, which documents the positioning the service provider would like to reach.

- *Strategy-formulation*: Positioning individual service segments in a single portfolio allows strategies to be pooled, which results in recommendations for long-term involvement in the service segment. The goal is to transform the actual portfolio with appropriate strategies into the target portfolio. Some portfolio approaches are already equipped with standard strategies, for example, investment and growth strategies, absorption and divestment strategies or selective strategies [Hinterhuber 1992]. The standard strategies must be supplemented with single strategy elements in individual cases.

- *Coordination of Portfolio, Development, and Production Strategies*: The coordination of Portfolio, Development, and Production strategies is crucial for strategic success, because all three strategies influence each other. Suppose, for example, a service provider performs a business environment analysis as a part of its Delivery Strategy. If this analysis reveals an intensified customer demand for Internet solutions, then the decision can be made within the Delivery Strategy to construct a product segment "Internet Solutions" (see Fig. 49). The consequence for Portfolio Strategy is, for example, that two new service segments "Internet Access" and "Email Service" must be strategically developed. This decision again has direct effects on Development and Production Strategies. A fitting development strategy may be to develop Internet-based solutions based on Microsoft.NET frameworks. This only makes sense when Intel/Microsoft-based server platforms are strongly anchored in the Production Strategy.

- Practically speaking, such process-spanning strategic coordination occurs rarely. However, development architecture and platform decisions are made, for example, without considering the effects on production; or surplus capacities are built up in production because the Portfolio Strategy is unknown or insufficiently communicated.

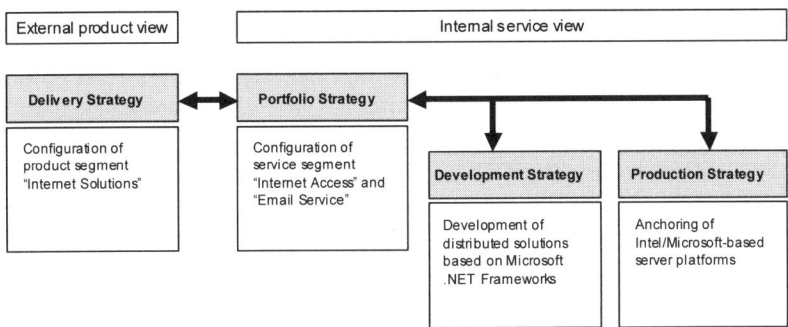

Fig. 49. Coordination of Delivery, Portfolio, Development, and Production Strategies

Portfolio Planning

The service segments identified in Portfolio Strategy are described more precisely in the context of Portfolio Planning. This will be done by planning the optimal service program and then defining the individual services. Portfolio Planning thus consists of the following two tasks:

- *Planning the service program*: The planning of the service program takes place on a tactical and an operational level. At a tactical level the most important objectives of the service program are planned. Thus the following questions must be answered [Schweitzer 1994]: Which services and service alternatives are to be manufactured internally or externally in what quantities and within which time frames? What new services are to be added to the service program in what quantities and within which time frames? Which and how many production plants are to be renewed within which time frames? Which services are to be developed within which time frames? How is the financial budget to be spent on investments and new services? Are the upper limits for service sales in the respective time frames reached or have sales fallen short?

  The answers to these questions result, in practice, in a dynamic optimization problem, because factors on both sides of the equation must be taken into consideration. Not only are sales factors shifting (e.g. demand and product life cycles), but internal factors (e.g. development, production, budget, and procurement constraints) are also changing.

  Operational service planning defines the exact production program for a given time frame (e.g. for one month or one year). It specifies the type, quality, and quantity of services to be produced.

  This results in a precisely formulated production order for the fixed period. In the service program's operational planning there are a set of numbers that must be accepted as given. This includes, for example, production capacities and procedures, product structures, sales and procurement upper limits, or financial budgets.

- *Service Planning*: The characteristics of each individual service must be defined in detail. There are two sets of figures which must be considered and incorporated. External customer requirements from Delivery Planning, above all the requirement analysis as defined within Requirement Management, must be integrated into the definitions. Conditions defined in the internal general framework and technological restrictions from development and production must also be taken into account.

  In addition to service functionality, quality criteria and resources required for the production of the service must be planned.

  Decisions on manufacturing depth, that means which parts of the service should be produced and which purchased, are to be met and coordinated with Sourcing Planning. The main result of Service Planning is the description of service characteristics in the form of a specification sheet. The specification sheet serves as basis for issuing a development order for the actual design and organization of the service.

Portfolio Controlling

Portfolio Controlling has the task of monitoring and steering the goals and objectives decided upon within Portfolio Planning. It must pay special attention to the efficient production of services, which guarantee a sustainable benefit to the customers' business processes. Portfolio Controlling must also monitor the investments made in IT infrastructure. Similar to Portfolio Planning, tasks can be grouped into the following two areas:

- *Service Program Controlling*: The planned service program must be continuously monitored. The production output quantities and time frames set in operational service program planning are subject to unexpected deviations due to various internal and external influencing factors. There can be, for example, delays in service development, production capacities can fail at short notice, or planned sales volumes can become unrealistic due to changed market conditions. Deviations must be identified as early as possible and negative effects minimized through service program modifications. For example, if service demand within a planned time frame falls shorter than expected, then other uses for freed production capacities must be explored. Or if a service loses its competitive edge earlier than planned, then potential follow-up services must be planned, developed, and brought on the market earlier than originally scheduled.

- *Service Controlling*: Each individual service must be monitored over its entire life cycle. The service monitoring begins with examination of the development of the service. In the same sense as that of project controlling, the development progress must be monitored with regard to quality, costs, and due dates. For existing services both market benchmarking figures, such as sales volumes and revenues, as well as internal key data, such as production costs and investments, must be continuously monitored. In this way, target/actual deviations can be identified quickly and appropriate measures taken. Again Service Controlling is dependent upon sales oriented input defined in Delivery Controlling and internal inputs on Development and Production Controlling. If deviations from planned key figures are identified, particularly those that are negative, then appropriate improvement measures are to be defined and initiated.

3.2.4.2 Development Management

Development is responsible for the design and organization of application systems. These activities are a central element of an IT service provider's production infrastructure, given that application systems steer the production process.

The application systems (i.e. development) have a significant impact on the functionality of IT services. However, decisions influencing IT service quality are made by production.

Based on the service characteristics, defined within Portfolio Planning and documented in the form of specification worksheets, services must be designed and drafted by the development unit. In practice, IT service providers' development focuses particularly on the design and organization of the required application systems.

Development Management tasks are, as in the other areas of integrated information management, grouped into strategic, planning, and controlling activities (see Fig. 50).

Development Strategy
• Development organization • Definition of development philosophies and standards • Strategic alignment of application portfolios • General framework for development tools and languages • Coordination of Portfolio, Development, and Production Strategies
Development Planning
• Project Planning • Resource Planning • Workload and cost planning • Development controlling planning • Coordination with technical production planning
Development Controlling
• Controlling development workloads • Development launch controlling • Support service controlling

Abb. 50. Development Management tasks

Development Strategy

The Development Strategy specifies the long-term, strategic general framework for the development process. It should cover the following tasks:

- *Development organization*: As a part of the IT service provider's organization in the context of Development Strategy, the development unit's structures and processes must be defined. Under the heading of processes, activities such as organizational positions, sets of responsibilities, disciplinary authority, as well as qualification profiles are to be specified [Balzert 1998]. Due to the fact that development is chiefly project driven, the definition of project forms and structures is a central task. In addition to the stable organizational process structures, development projects also frequently require temporary structural measures, for example for the development of new services. The definition and implementation of these temporary measures belong to development planning because they are not of a strategic nature. However, what are of increasing importance for development are strategies regarding so-called offshoring, i.e. the use or relocation of development resources to low-wage countries.

Apart from the fundamental decision for or against offshoring, which often must be decided in an overall business context, the smooth organizational realization and/or integration of external development units must be explicated in the development strategy.

Development organization follows a previously approved procedural or processing concept. There are many models available for precisely this purpose. The established concepts include, for example, the waterfall model, the v model, the spiral model, the object oriented model or rapid prototyping. This list grows constantly with new models, i.e. currently extreme programming or agile software development. In the context of Development Strategy the process model or models to be implemented are to be selected and adapted to individual needs.

- *Definition of development philosophies and standards*: Design philosophies and standards, which form a part of application architecture, are the foundation for application development. Design philosophies are universally valid principles which apply to the development process. One such application oriented design philosophy is, for example, the choice of client/server-based, web-based, or service oriented architecture. Likewise the design philosophy dictates how to organize application architecture, such as modularly, hierarchically, or distributed. Thereby modular organization of application architectures is becoming increasingly a mainstream design philosophy, because it enables the reusability of previously constructed solutions.

   Design philosophies must be created and followed under the concept of "Design for Production," i.e. they must be directed toward an economically efficient production of IT services.

   The decision on how to deal with standard software or individual software is another important element in the design philosophy. Fig. 51 illustrates what such a design philosophy can look like, such that the main types of customer applications are defined in strategically strived-for application categories. For the earlier development phases, philosophies and principles should also be specified, such as those with respect to concepts and methods for object oriented analysis or for software ergonomics.

When implementing design philosophies, usually precise standards can be used. Thus web-based application architectures can be realized with known Microsoft.Net or J2EE standards. Service oriented architectures require a middleware. Here too there are different standards and solutions available. The same applies to standards for designing user front-ends or safety architecture. The central development standards are to be specified in the context of Development Strategy.

Category Type	Client/server applications	Web applications	(Single) workplace applications	Host applications
Standard software	SAP (ERP)	Web link to standard software	MS Office	replace
Individual software (externally developed)	if required, possible	Target architecture	if required, possible	replace
Internal development (standard components and individual software)	if required, possible	Target architecture	if required, possible	replace
Legacy Systems	not applicable	not applicable	not applicable	replace

☐ = Strategic target segments

Fig. 51. Illustrative strategy for implementing diverse application architectures [Source ITMC AG, Horgen]

- *Strategic alignment of application portfolios*: Service providers are usually running many application systems at the same time, which support the production of various IT services. Applications portfolios, like service portfolios, must be strategically planned.

  The application portfolio must be designed and steered with respect to life cycle characteristics.

  This entails, for example, a consistent separation of data and functions, which can be achieved through the development of independent application systems for the preparation of data. Application architecture describes the service provider's target application portfolio. The description is based on both a business oriented and technical understanding. The business oriented view serves in defining the target functionality of applications related to the customer's business processes. The technical view presents the systems from the perspective of service production with all of its components, coordination, as well as its data relevant integration. Newly developed application systems are to be integrated into the application portfolio. At the same time, architecture found in the existing application portfolio must be evaluated regularly.

- *General framework for development tools and languages*: Suitable development tools (CASE tools) are necessary to support professional software development. These tools are used in the early planning, definition, and design phases, as well as, in the later implementation, test and introduction phases. Philosophies and standards specified in the strategy have influence on the choice of development tools. In the context of Development Strategy, tools must not be selected based on a great amount of detail, but instead a strategic general framework concerning tool platform or tool supplier choices must be defined. The same applies for the choice of development languages.

- *Coordination of Portfolio, Development, and Production Strategies*: See the description under Portfolio Strategy

Development Planning

In the context of Development Planning, the planning of the development workload is specified precisely. Planning is specifically focused on three dimensions, namely, Project Planning, Resource Planning, and Cost Planning. Furthermore, the controlling system for development must be planned. This results in the following tasks:

- *Project Planning*: A project plan refines and details tasks, phases, and milestones of a development project on the basis of the processing concept specified within development strategy [Balzert 1998]. In addition, tasks are usually delegated to employees in the context of Project Planning. There are many well-known methods available for Project Planning (e.g. network plans or Gantt diagrams) and tools (e.g. Microsoft Project).

- *Resource Planning*: Resources are necessary for the realization of development projects. The resources must be planned in order to minimize unexpected shortages or excess capacities. In development, resources are essentially those of personnel and capital equipment (hardware, software). With respect to time, these resources must be distributed among the various development projects as optimally as possible. When planning personnel resources, attributes such as qualification, available capacity, temporal availability, physical location, and organizational situation must be considered [Balzert 1998]. In planning capital equipment, various established methods and procedures are available. Examples of capital equipment characteristics to be considered are development workplaces, development and test platforms, and also office space and materials.

- *Workload and Cost Planning*: Development costs represent a major share of the total costs of an IT service. In IT, development costs are mainly those spent on personnel. Therefore, in an initial step, the expected personnel expenditure for a development project can be estimated. For the workload expenditure estimation, many procedures have been developed in the past. These basically estimate the temporal personnel expenditure for the production of new, or the modification of existing applications. In the context of Cost Planning, these expenditures are estimated in monetary terms. Other expenditures (e.g. for software licenses, development systems, or test systems) are planned as either independent service types or converted into person days.

- *Development Controlling Planning*: A number of planning tasks must be carried out when controlling development projects [Balzert 1998]. This includes, for example, the development of quantity and quality standards, the definition of quality assurance methods, and the development of productivity, quality, and process metrics. Control and reporting systems must be established, for example budget summaries, project progress reports, or due date reviews. Measurement and auditing procedures (software metrics) for development processes and products must be defined.

- *Coordination with technical production planning*: Early on, development and production departments must coordinate their planning activities. Development and production have different goals and cost structures, which, if planned independently, will cause problems. These problems must be analyzed and then solved within the context of Portfolio Strategy.

    Between Development Planning and Production Planning there are many interdependencies, which can only be managed by complementary planning.

    The construction of qualitative and quantitative production capacities must be planned in such a way that the capacities are available by the time the development project is completed and thus needs them. Then again, development needs concrete information about the planned states of production in order to be able to align their project activities accordingly.

Development Controlling

Development Controlling concentrates on the following three tasks:

- *Controlling development workloads*: Projects, resources, and costs must be monitored continuously. Here Development Planning presents the foundation for Development Controlling. Based on the reporting systems and metrics defined there, measurements can be taken, deviations identified, and corrective actions initiated.

- *Development launch controlling*: New or modified application systems must be taken into production. The launch follows a given process, which must be controlled by development. In the context of a launch, all characteristics of an application system must be verified. This applies to training as well.

- *Support service controlling*: The majority of support incidents are dealt with within the context of production controlling. However, again and again it happens that these problems are due to incorrectly developed application systems. For these instances corrective maintenance of application systems must adhere to an explicitly described support process, which must exist within development. This process should contain, as in production, a problem management and change management process. Establishing a configuration management is instrumental within this framework, in that it enables an explicit management of all software elements, software versions, and software modifications.

3.2.4.3 Production Management

IT products result from the production of IT services. In addition to the management of service portfolios and the management of service development, real production, i.e. the production of IT services, must be planned, executed, and controlled.

The management of production is an independent task, which the service provider must actively be engaged in.

All units involved in the production of a service must be consulted with on Production Planning, Steering, and Controlling and their effect on business [Heinen 1991]. In IT production, production infrastructure typically consists of central elements, which are thought of in combination with a computing center (e.g. server or storage systems), decentralized elements which are operated at the service customer's location (e.g. workplace systems or printers), or the connections between central and decentralized elements (e.g. networks). Analogous to industrial manufacturing, different production types exist within IT production. Batch production and online production are the most obvious and significant types. Their respective characteristics have a significant impact on the concrete arrangement of organizational production processes and structures.

IT services can be produced in different ways, i.e. on different production platforms.

The list of tasks for Production Management covers both long-term structural decisions, as well as mid- and short-term tasks regarding Production Planning and Controlling (see Fig. 52).

Production Strategy

An essential prerequisite for production efficiency is the presence of a Production Strategy and its coordination with the service provider's other strategies. This applies in particular to the long-term planning of production infrastructure, which in industrial manufacturing is also known as plant engineering.

Within the context of Production Strategy, special attention must be given to strategic cost management.

The Production Strategy definition covers the following tasks:

- *Organization of production*: Just as in the Development Strategy, also in the context of the Production Strategy, structural decisions are to be made concerning the organization of production. Next to questions of structure and process organization in production, the spatial organization of production plants (layout planning) plays a central role, in addition to decisions on procurement of individual production plants, their capacity characteristics, and questions about a maintenance strategy. Regarding spatial planning, plans must be thought through with respect to, for example: how servers are to be arranged; the wiring and network requirements; the electrical sources; temperature requirements; the physical entrance systems; requirements on air purity or radiation effects [OGC 2002]. Decisions on individual production plants, for instance the purchase of a mainframe, and its capacity characteristics are usually made on a long-term basis and thus must be strategically planned.

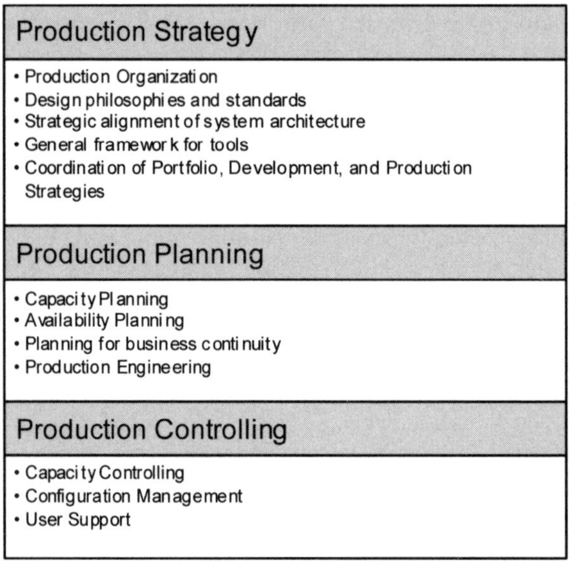

Production Strategy
- Production Organization
- Design philosophies and standards
- Strategic alignment of system architecture
- General framework for tools
- Coordination of Portfolio, Development, and Production Strategies

Production Planning
- Capacity Planning
- Availability Planning
- Planning for business continuity
- Production Engineering

Production Controlling
- Capacity Controlling
- Configuration Management
- User Support

Fig. 52. Production Management tasks

- *Design philosophies and standards*: The organization of production infrastructure should take place on the basis of selected principles and standards.

  Production has its own design tasks, which must realized independently.

  For example, it must be explicitly specified how modular, scalable, flexible, secure, or error tolerant the infrastructure needs to be. To this end, the existing standards (e.g. hardware or platform standards) can be used. Here the already mentioned coordination of development and production standards is important.

- *Strategic alignment of system architecture*: The architecture defines the long-term design of production infrastructure in the sense of a blueprint. Architectures should be premeditated, to the extent necessary, for all elements of the infrastructure. This includes, for example, architectures for central servers and host systems, networks, client systems, mobile devices, storage systems, printers or backup and recovery systems.

- *General framework for tools*: Various software tools are available for controlling and monitoring production. There are strategic objectives and fundamental requirements placed on tools. These descriptions must be laid out in the Production Strategy.

- *Coordination of Portfolio, Development, and Production Strategies*: See the description under Portfolio Strategy

Production Planning

The planning of IT production is concerned with both the organization of IT production infrastructure and the planning of IT production execution, i.e. the production processes. With the organization of IT infrastructure the prerequisites for the execution of production tasks are fulfilled. The cost structures and basis for the quality of production are specified here. Similar to the principles of "plant engineering," this follows from the development of architectures, the definition of data models and automation instruments, as well as the definition of standards. Production Planning takes place on the basis of the current production program that was defined in the context of Portfolio Planning. Production Planning covers all planning tasks which guarantee, under the constant aspect of economical efficiency, the provision of production-suitable IT services. The following described tasks are ITIL Best Practices oriented (see Chapter 2.6). For this reason only some—from our viewpoint—central aspects are pointed out here:

- *Capacity Planning*: The core element of production planning is Capacity Planning. The most important task is to coordinate, as optimally as possible, capacity requirements and available capacity. The expected capacity requirements result from the previously defined production program, i.e. the type and quantity of services to be produced within a given time frame. Every service to be produced requires certain production resources (e.g. computers, memory, and transmission resources). For example, if a service provider knows it must produce 150 000 salary statements in one month, the required production capacity for these IT services can be estimated from this fact. However, a prerequisite is that production resources required for one salary statement are computed as precisely as possible. This task is accomplished in industrial manufacturing through the evaluation of parts lists. In IT production, parts lists are more or less unknown. In IT production, only rarely is a real Capacity Planning undertaken, the reason being that usually, in practice, each new IT service gets its own new production infrastructure. Thus, for example, each application system runs on a separate server. New servers are ordered for new applications. Therefore, substantial over-capacities exist because computers are not operating anywhere near their full capacity. Our discussions with computing center managers show that such over-capacities can lie in and around 30–60% of total capacity, particularly in the area of Open Systems.

This procedure will change with the current virtualization of IT production resources. Today computer, memory, and network resources can be supplied on demand and be installed for the production of various IT services. In this context, Capacity Planning will play a crucial role in the efficiency and effectiveness of production. Over-capacities (e.g. computers not working at full capacity) lead to inefficiencies, and under-capacities usually lead to quality deficits, for example regarding response times). A unique challenge for IT Capacity Planning lies in the strong temporal fluctuations of service demand. Thus, for example, in the course of a day there are peaks of demand for certain IT services, like checking emails or logging in at the beginning of the working day or after lunch. The same applies to the period at the year's end, in which, for example, production demand peaks for end-of-year or personnel accounting statements. Such demand fluctuations must be considered in Capacity Planning. However, this does not mean that today's common practice in IT production of defining production capacity based on the expected peak is correct.

- *Availability Planning*: Availability is one of the main quality criteria of IT services from a service customer's point of view. Availability has a significant impact on how satisfied service customers are with IT services. This is the reason the dimension of availability is usually defined very precisely in SLAs, which are the sealed contracts with service customers. Availability Planning must guarantee that the agreed availability ratios are kept all of the time. While for service customers only the service's entire availability is relevant, within the context of Availability Planning the responsible units of IT production must be identified and organized. These are the actual components of production infrastructure (e.g. servers or networks) in addition to production, maintenance, and support processes. Thus, for example, while for a service customer—based on his job—only the availability of email services is relevant, Availability Planning must determine which requirements are to be placed on servers, networks, data bases, and backup systems, so that the guaranteed availability ratio can be maintained.

An inadequate Availability Planning leads to promised availability ratios not being kept. Often IT units have no comprehension how high the costs of this unavailability actually are. One must consider that not only material damages result—in the form of employee productivity losses, revenue losses, penalties, or overtime—but also intangible damages such as customer dissatisfaction, potential customer and business losses, damages to image, or loss of confidence. Both for the service provider and service customer these losses, in turn, can result in even further unforeseeable costs.

In the context of Availability Planning several tasks must be performed. These include determining the availability requirements of service customers, the consequences of the promised availability defined in the final SLA, and creating availability monitoring and reporting systems.

- *Planning for business continuity:* In many companies IT services have a great impact on business processes. This makes it necessary to develop emergency plans, which guarantee a predefined level of service should single components of production infrastructure fail or in the case of a total production crash. A continuity strategy must be developed with information delivered from a business impact analysis and a risk analysis. In a business impact analysis critical business processes are identified and the consequences of a loss of these business processes are analyzed. In a risk analysis the probability and the effects of serious incidents (e.g. natural catastrophes, terrorist attacks) are assessed. The continuity strategy should include measures for both minimizing risks and organizational and technical mechanisms for re-establishing production readiness after an emergency. The latter usually includes a clear prioritization of the IT services which must be made available in case of an emergency. When an emergency occurs, the continuity strategy is to be implemented and monitored continuously.

- *Production Engineering:* Production prepares production know-how for other units in the form of a "technical center of excellence." In addition to creating technical studies and concepts, such as with regard to new manufacturing technologies or platforms, this center of excellence offers support to the other units. The center can take on an advisory function in projects, such as those involving the introduction of new infrastructures or developing new services. The center can also support the day-in, day-out work, for example with respect to problem solution within user support or monitoring production infrastructure.

Production Controlling

The operational Production Controlling is responsible for the continuous monitoring of production procedures. Production Controlling with respect to Capacity Controlling has the task to tune, making fine adjustments to production capacities. This means in detail:

- *Capacity Controlling:* In contrast to Capacity Planning, which is based on a medium-term time frame, Capacity Controlling has a short-term character. Short-term production program changes and fluctuations have a continuous influence on capacity requirements. For example, if the demand for an IT product is less than expected, then freed production capacities can be used for other purposes at short notice, if necessary. The same applies to the reverse case of unexpectedly high demand. In this case, Capacity Controlling must provide for a short-term supply of additional capacities. Also the failure of individual production resources, like a server or hard disk, may require a reallocation of capacities. If additional or new IT services must be produced at short notice, it is the task of Capacity Controlling to pull this off with the existing production program.

- *Configuration Management:* The production infrastructure must be continuously monitored at both the level of IT services and at the level of individual production resources. This applies in particular to those elements of the production infrastructure which have an effect on the agreed SLA. This monitoring and controlling takes place in the context of Configuration Management. Configuration Management is built up from a Configuration Management Database, in which all relevant components and information are documented (see Chapter 2.5 and Ex. 5). If plan deviations are detected, they must be analyzed and improvement measures initiated, for example tuning measures.

- *User Support:* User Support must also be ensured in the context of Production Controlling. Practically speaking, support processes are usually closely tied to ITIL Best Practices (see Chapter 2.6). User inquiries are collected and managed with the help of an incident management process. If incident management cannot solve the problem, it is given over to a 2nd-level support. This 2nd-level support identifies the underlying problem in a Problem Management process. In a Change Management process a solution is constructed and implemented with the help of a Release Management process. When necessary additional units, such as development, must be consulted in the sense of a 3rd-level support.

4 Practical Examples of Integrated Information Management

In this chapter, based on selected examples, we would like to show what integrated information management signifies in practical terms and how individual elements of the presented model can be implemented. The examples presented here deal with projects, on which the "Integrated Information Management" Competence Center collaborated with its partner companies. The project results presented here are at least partially anonymous for reasons of privacy or redefined with fictitious numbers.

4.1 Six Sigma Analysis of IT Production Processes[1]

Six Sigma enjoys increasing popularity as a method for Quality Management. More and more companies are acknowledging the advantages of this method and submitting their processes to Six Sigma Analysis. Earlier there had been a long-standing bias against Six Sigma in that it was thought to be exclusively for manufacturing companies with standardized, highly repetitive manufacturing processes [Schmutte 2002]. However, in the meanwhile this opinion has changed due to successful Six Sigma projects in service companies.

Six Sigma Analysis is suitable for information management processes too. This applies particularly to production processes, less to planning and development processes. The reason for this is that IT production processes are service processes and exhibit typical characteristics of industrial manufacturing processes. These processes are, to a high degree, standardized and, to a high degree, exhibit repetition frequency. In a pilot project we examined the relevance of the Six Sigma method for IT production processes. The project concentrated on an analysis of the support process of a big, data intensive application of one of our research partners. Here the project procedure and selected project results are presented. However, first we present a short introduction to the basics of Six Sigma methods.

4.1.1 Six Sigma Basics

In practice different approaches are hidden behind the buzzword Six Sigma. These vary from a purely methodical procedure for improvement projects to a company-wide development philosophy [Schmutte 2002]. The Motorola company devel-

---

[1] The information presented in this chapter is based on research by Axel Hochstein, Institute for Information Management at the University of St. Gallen.

oped Six Sigma in the 1980s for the quality assurance of production processes. The objective of Six Sigma is to create stable and manageable processes. Stable and manageable means that the process results (process outputs) are subject to as small as possible fluctuations and that these fluctuations lie within customer-given tolerance ranges. For this purpose Six Sigma utilizes simple statistical instruments. Customers define upper and lower tolerance limits for process results. For example, customers define the maximum deviation of a drilled hole in a given production process. If the tolerance limit for the drilled hole is 0.1 mm, then the process quality for the customer is no longer acceptable whenever a drilling deviates by more than 0.1 mm from the customer required dimension.

Within a Six Sigma Analysis, the process is then statistically evaluated, in that both the mathematical average and the standard deviation (sigma) of the process results are calculated. The process stability can be expressed with the sigma level, i.e. the degree of deviation of process results from their average value. More precisely, Six Sigma stability means that after having completed 1 million processes, the result—statistically evaluated—is only 3.4 times outside of the tolerance range specified by the customer (see Fig. 53). In relation to the previous example, drilled holes may deviate at most 3.4 times by more than 0.1 mm from the customer-defined dimension after having completed 1 million drillings. A company's target must not necessarily be that of the Six Sigma quality level. Investigations show that in fact companies on the average reach a level of 4-Sigma in their production processes, i.e. having completed 1 million process runs, the process result is 6210 times outside of the tolerance range. It is to note, however, that already with a quality level of 4-Sigma, quality costs make up approximately 15–25% of revenue.

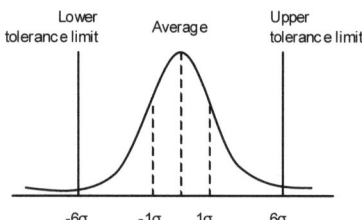

	Process Sigma	Rate of errors per million processes	Quality costs (as a % of revenue)
Not competitive	2	308537	Not acceptable
Average	4	6210	15-25%
World class	6	3.4	<1%

Fig. 53. The Six Sigma method

The end goal of a Six Sigma analysis is to align the processes of a company to its customers' requirements. Methodically, Six Sigma is based on two basic components:

- A *strictly systematic procedure* based on quantitative, statistical instruments, which covers in particular a precise measurement of process quality, but also the analysis, improvement, and control of processes
- A *training and coaching methodology*, which ensures that the necessary know-how in executing Six Sigma projects is available throughout the company

Six Sigma assures a systematic course of action by employing a DMAIC cycle (see Fig. 54). This differentiates between five phases: Define, Measure, Analyze, Improve, and Control. Specific tools and instruments are available for each phase. A detailed description of the five phases is presented by way of an example.

The training and coaching methodology is based on the so-called Belt Concept. Similar to Asian martial arts, Six Sigma defines clear roles and responsibilities (e.g. Black Belt or Green Belt). The participants go through a training program of several weeks and are at the same time involved in current Six Sigma projects. A graduate of the highest level of education is certified with a Six Sigma Black Belt. If a company defines Six Sigma as a part of the business philosophy, then in practice this frequently implies that starting at some level of management, certain Six Sigma Belts must be acquired.

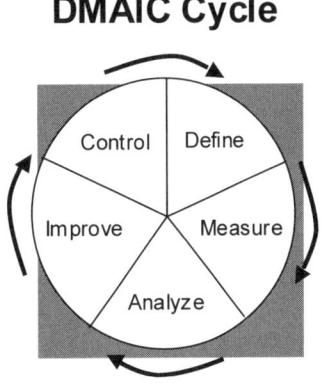

Phase	Tool, Instrument
D	SIPOC, CTQ, VOC, Stakeholder Analysis, Rolled Through put Yield
M	Kano Model, Gage R&R, Prioritization Matrix, Process Capability, Process Sigma
A	Affinity Diagram, Stratified Frequency Plot, Hypothesis Test, Scatter Plot, Regression, Cause-and-Effect Diagram
I	FMEA, Pareto Chart, Design of Experiments, Sampling, CoPQ
C	Data Collection Plan, Quality Control Process Chart, Control Charts, Standardization

Fig. 54. Phases of the DMAIC cycle

4.1.2 Six Sigma Analysis of IT Application Support

In a pilot project the support process for a big application was examined together with one of the Competence Center's research partners. The chosen application was a host-based legacy application for the support of a company core business process. The application was used by approx. 23 000 users and has turned out to be a support-intensive application. Daily approximately 300 inquiries were made to the Help Desk, each resulting in the creation a new ticket. 70% of the tickets could be resolved by 1st-level support (first solution rate). Approximately 300 problem reports were created weekly, which were handled in 2nd- or 3rd-level support.

With the help of the Six Sigma Analysis the following targets should have been reached:

- A *measurable improvement of the quality of the support process* (improvement of the first solution rate, response time, etc.)

- A *measurable improvement of the quality of the application system* (reduction in number of tickets and problem reports)

- A *measurable reduction of the cost of the support process* (reduction in number of tickets as well as cost for each ticket)

The list below contains fictitious quantitative values, for reasons of confidentiality, and is not correlated with the actual values.

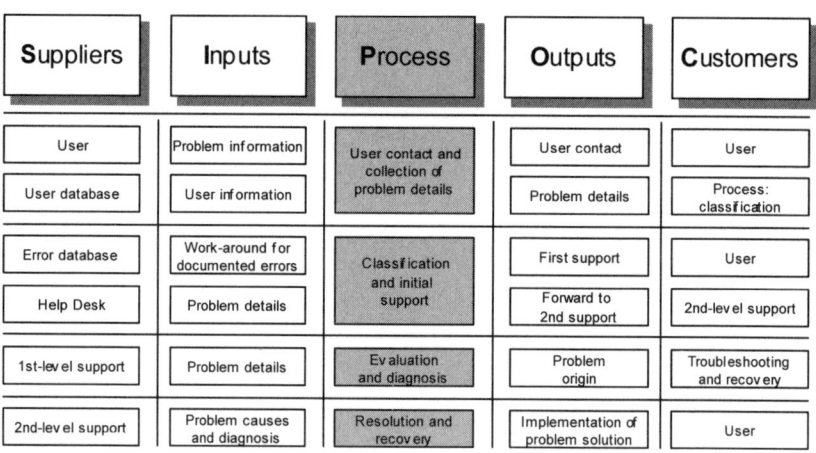

Fig. 55. High-level SIPOC diagram of the support processes

Define Phase

The project procedure followed the DMAIC cycle. The central point of the Define Phase was not only project definition and project setup but also, more importantly, the to-be-improved process definition and description. This included establishing customer quality criteria and tolerance limits. The SIPOC diagram was used as an instrument for describing processes. In the SIPOC diagram, the individual process-step definitions take into account suppliers, inputs, outputs, and customers. The SIPOC diagram presented in Fig. 55 illustrates the results of the support process at the highest level. Each of the four subprocesses can be broken down further into more detailed activities (not presented here).

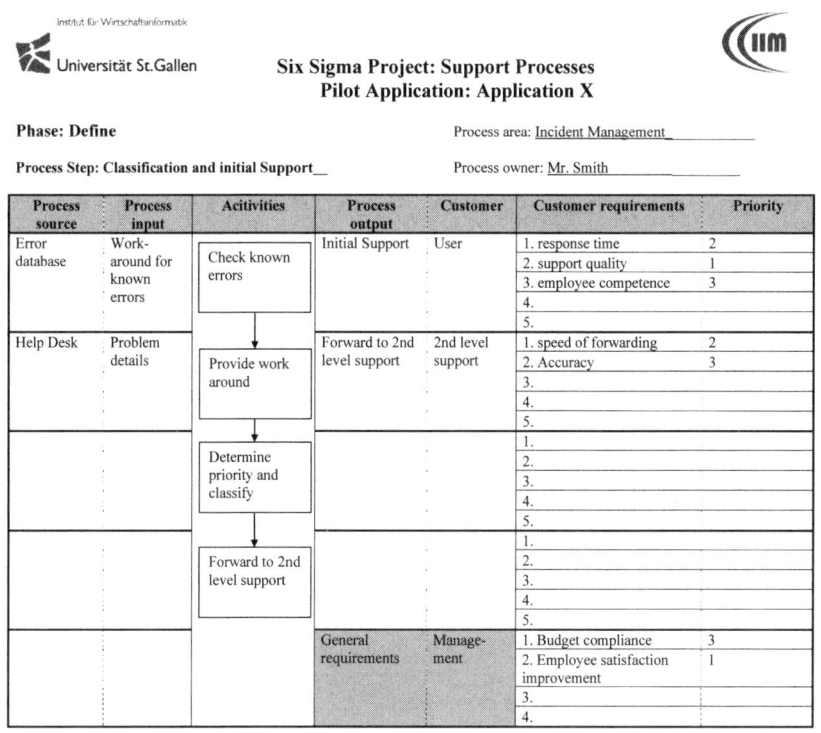

Fig. 56. Classification and Initial Support process step requirements (extract)

One of the main prerequisites for a Six Sigma process analysis is having established the customer process requirements. Requirements from a customer perspective must be defined for the results of each process step and each activity. These requirements are also called Critical to Quality (CTQ) and can be established with different methods (e.g. customer interviews, questionnaires, customer complaints, customer segmenting, or brainstorming). Fig. 56 presents customer requirements for the first two activities using the process step Classification and First Support. The requirements were additionally evaluated with respect to their importance from a customer perspective. Next to activity-related requirements, there are also general requirements for every process step. These deal mainly with management requirements.

Measure Phase

In the Measure Phase the customer requirements for a process identified in the Define Phase are measured. The objective is to determine the current level of quality for each requirement. For this purpose the Measure Phase covers the following activities:

- Institutionalizing the identified requirement criteria

- Definition of a suitable measuring method and a representative random sampling size

- Measurement of current quality using new method and requirement criteria

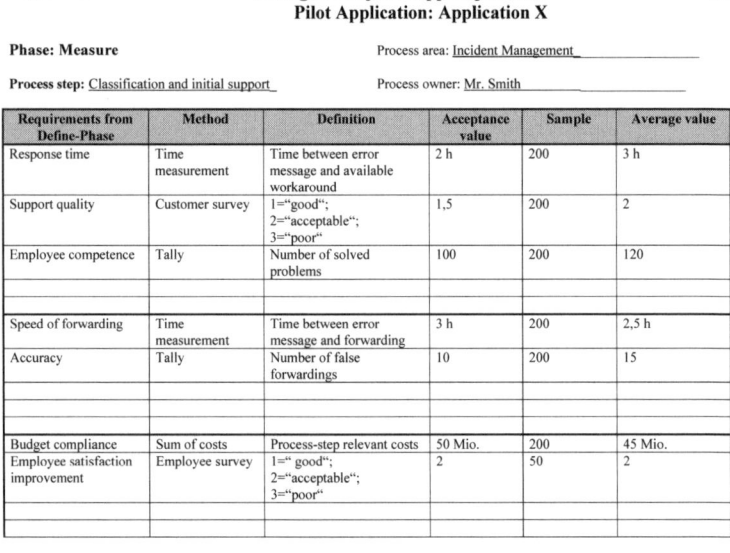

Fig. 57. Measure Phase results (extract)

In Fig. 57 the results of the Measure Phase for the process step Classification and First Support are presented. The requirement criteria formulated in the Define Phase are refined with individual specifications of measuring method, measuring unit, user acceptance value, and random sampling size. The results are given as the average measured value (mathematical average) and the sigma level (standard deviation).

Analyze Phase

Of all of the criteria, response time, employee competence, and budget compliance exhibit the lowest sigma levels. This shows that the processes based on their results are subject to great fluctuations in quality. The roots and actual causes of the low level of quality must be investigated in the Analyze Phase. The verification of causes should be based first and foremost on concrete data.

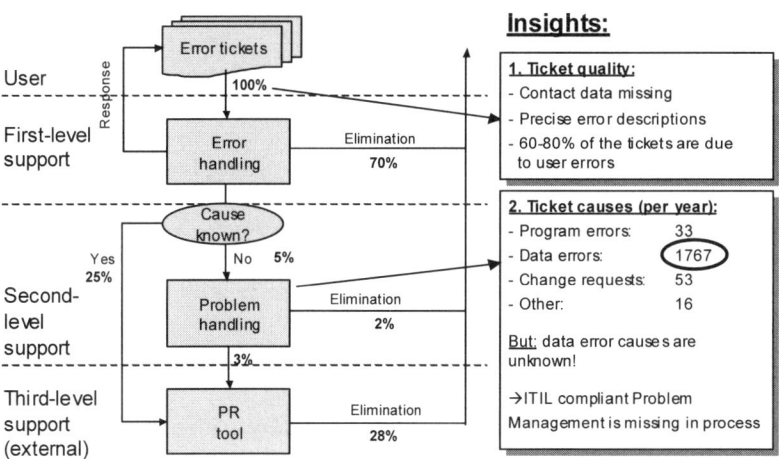

Fig. 58. Cause analysis within the Analyze Phase

The two main problem areas were identified as ticket quality and ticket cause (see Fig. 58). The quality of ticket information was bad. In particular user contact data was frequently missing, which often resulted in complex and arduous tasks of reconstruction. 60–80% of all tickets were the result of user errors. In 2nd-level support the ticket causes were analyzed. The result of this analysis proved that approximately 95% of all tickets were due to data errors. The cause of many data errors remained unknown because even after much evaluation very few verifiable conclusions could be made. Some presumed reasons include, for example, data inconsistencies, which were the result of updates or conversions or incorrectly entered data. Moreover, in the analysis it was found that an ITIL compliant problem management process, practically speaking, did not exist. One result of this was that in the context of 2nd-level support only visible errors were repaired, whereas actual error causes were insufficiently analyzed.

Improve and Control Phase

The last two phases of the DMAIC cycle are not specifically Six Sigma, which is why they will only be dealt with briefly here. In the Improve Phase possible solutions are sought, which should help eliminate the actual cause of the poor quality. Typically, several alternatives are developed and evaluated. In this pilot project the solutions focused primarily on the implementation of a Best Practice based on ITIL for the support process.

The monitoring of the improvement measures implementation, as well as the continuous monitoring of process quality are tasks dealt with in the Control Phase.

4.2 Integrated Cost Accounting and IT Products[2]

The demand for process-supporting IT products, e.g. the "Invoice Billing" or "Processing a Booking Transaction," is increasing. An IT service provider, which would like to offer such products, must be able to make these entire calculations in advance and settle the relevant accounts continuously. Frequently even a unit based cost calculation is demanded. What many customers want to know today is, at what unit price can, for example, a salary statement be produced or a booking transaction processed. The accompanying question is then how these prices vary at different levels of quantities purchased.

Today many IT service providers do not have cost-computational instruments to calculate unit cost prices of process-supporting IT products and thus to charge accordingly. They do not know their actual product production costs, which in turn makes price negotiations more difficult, if not impossible, with customers in competition-intense market segments.

In this context there are two problems which can be seen as causes. First of all there is an absence of cost calculation models, which enable an accurate mapping of technical cost categories to business process-supporting IT products as cost objects. Many service providers are not able to assess the requirements of the various technical service objects, for example computing power, memory, or transmission rates necessary for an individual IT product. Secondly, today in

---

[2] The information presented in this chapter is based on research by Jochen Scheeg, Deutsche Telekom AG.

practice development and production costs are taken into account in a more or less isolated fashion. This applies to both cost planning and cost accounting. Independent of each other, development and production units have relationships with their joint customer pools and apply different cost objects. While in development, for example, application systems and development projects serve as cost objects, production typically uses hardware or transaction related cost objects. This isolated cost perspective makes an IT product's life cycle oriented cost planning and accounting more difficult. Business process-supporting IT products require both development and production services. A prerequisite for a service provider's calculation of such products is thus an integrated cost perspective.

Following we present the fundamentals of a solution for the calculation of business process supporting IT products. Incorporating development and production costs, this approach allows for the calculation of product unit costs. In addition to this solution concept, an implementation prototype is presented, which was built on the basis of SAP R/3 in cooperation with the system integrator and consulting firm Syskoplan. However, first we will shortly summarize the state of affairs of cost accounting in IT development and IT production.

4.2.1 Status Quo in IT Cost Accounting

Status Quo in IT Development

IT development is made up of predominantly human resource services. The activities cover all stages of software development, from analysis, through draft (design) and programming, up to and including testing application systems. The dominant measurements are time units, measured in hours or days. The central service categories are concepts, system descriptions, projects, programs, or application systems. The cost objects, projects, application systems, and orders usually represent those services which are defined in IT development offerings or sales agreements.

In the past various procedures were developed to estimate the cost of IT development services, each taking into account a variety of influential factors [Balzert 2000]. Function Point and Constructive Cost Model (Cocomo) procedures are among the most well known. All procedures aim at determining the resource expenditure for producing a new application system and/or changing an existing application system. These procedures focus essentially on the estimation of the temporal human resource expenditure. Afterwards this expenditure is converted into monetary terms. Other expenditures, such as software licenses, development systems, or test systems, are offered to customers either as independent services or converted into service developer or person days.

Tools are often implemented for estimating costs, which are usually not embedded in the IT development's cost calculation systems. An inclusion of some plan data into bookkeeping systems usually only occurs at the customer's insistence. Today,

IT development's cost accounting systems are primarily used for cost registration and settlement.

Fig. 59 illustrates the prevailing accounting logic for IT development services. The cost centers of the cross-sectional units (development support) are compensated according to recorded temporal expenditures or by reallocation to cost centers in service production (application development). The application development expenditures are charged to projects (here: orders) according to their time expenditure. The cost objects are charged their order costs by means of an order accounting. Each company must individually specify the design and organization of the individual economic units to be subject to costs, such as cost centers, orders, or cost objects.

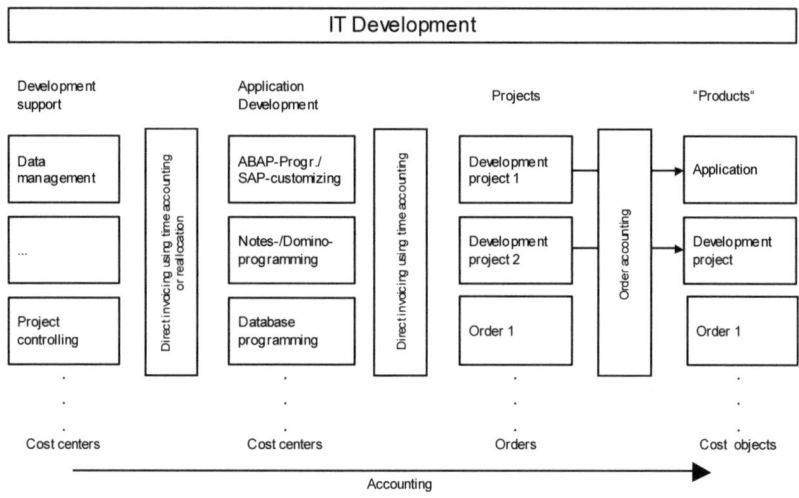

Fig. 59. Accounting logic in IT development

In conclusion it can be stated that an IT service provider is considered successful if it provides the defined quality with planned resources in the planned time frame. The efficient use of production resources for the developed service is of secondary importance. This means that the expected IT production costs in application system development play only a subordinate role, although the type and quantity of resources required for IT production, to a large extent, defined at the end of software development. Costs can only be marginally affected within IT production, through optimization measures.

Status Quo in IT Production

IT production provides both computing and human resource services. The computing services include processing, memory, and data transmission; the human resource services include management of the technical infrastructure. The computing services are of greater significance and are technically defined. Typical measurement factors in computer processing are CPU seconds or millions of instructions per second (MIPS). Data storage is measured in gigabytes. Data transmission is measured in either the bandwidth of the available transmission capacity or by the quantity of data transmitted. Service types are categorized as processing, storing, or transferring data. Cost objects can be differentiated in definition and structuring as either those with (direct) service category character (e.g. application transactions or use of hardware resources) or cost objects which are related to order definition (e.g. business units or application systems) [Mai 1996].

In estimating costs, the estimation of the infrastructure resources necessary to run the application systems is of central importance. The possibilities to estimate costs range from simple rules of thumb, trend analyses, analytic and simulation models up to complex benchmarking. The increasing complexity allows for more precise estimations, though it also entails greater financial effort.

Despite the methodical basis and multitude of possibilities for resource estimation, most service providers make these calculations only with regard to host computers and when employing standard software. Special software tools (sizing tools) are, for example, available for defining the necessary dimensions of the infrastructure required for SAP R/3 applications and Oracle databases. Based on empirical evidence of IT service production, the dimensions of the production infrastructure can be forecast using customers propositions as to the intensity of use and temporal use processing. It is uncommon to see this type of estimation in either Unix or Windows environments. Instead, should it become apparent that dimensions are too small, capacity would be increased as necessary.

Fig. 60 shows today's most prevalent accounting logic for IT service production. The support cost centers are compensated either through a direct accounting or a reallocation to a hardware position. These services are grouped and/or combined into intermediate products. Intermediate products are those services which, based on accounting data, can be charged directly to cost objects, and thus to the services of IT production. If a cost object is a technically defined entity, then there is a simple direct allocation from the type of service to the cost object. If cost object definitions involve customer or business process orientation, then a bundling of different service types occurs. As in IT development, each company must individually specify the design and organization of the individual economic units to be subject to costs.

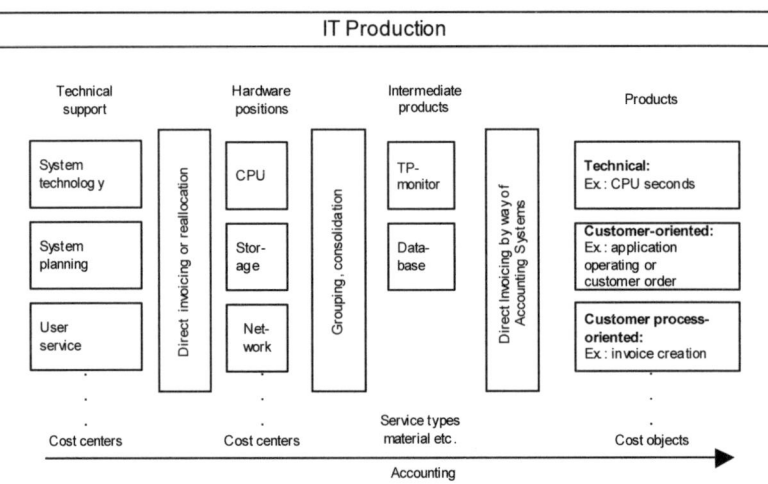

Fig. 60. Accounting logic in IT production

In the past few years, due to the extraordinary fixed cost problem within IT production, the existing IT production cost accounting systems have been extended to include elements of process cost calculation. Processes necessary for the production of individual services, with their associated process costs, are allocated to the individual activity centers. By way of a defined "Cost Driver," similar to the accounting of the service types in the traditional cost calculation, process costs are assigned to the cost objects [Fuerer 1994].

In conclusion it can be stated that a primary goal of IT production is the optimization of costs of employed production resources. Typical characteristics of IT production benchmarks verify this, for example costs per MIPS or costs per GB. These characteristics do not refer to the service provider's output as a whole (i.e. to the support of business processes by IT services) but instead provide information about the costs incurred in processing output. The effectiveness of creating whole IT services is not taken into consideration. From the IT production standpoint there is a simple reason for this: Its influence on application development platform and architecture definitions and, in the long run, the actual implementation is very limited.

Conclusion and Evaluation

The above observations about the status quo give evidence of the existence of effective cost computational tools for both IT development and IT production. However, a systematic cost-related integration—in the sense of a life cycle oriented product view—is missing. This poses the threat of inefficiencies in service production, which have essentially three origins:

- Due to their separate delivery and service relationships with their joint customers, in the past IT development and IT production each established their own specific service definitions. Today a common service definition integrating the services of development and production exists, if at all, only rudimentarily in accounting and is not at all temporally congruent with planning.
- The consequence of the missing integration is that there is no obligation to coordinate development and production, although only together can they be of genuine use to the customer. The mutual dependence and optimization potential has, to a great extent, been ignored in product planning.
- In order to be able to identify optimization potential in the coordination of development and production, it is necessary already in the service planning phase to evaluate the computational costs of all alternatives. Although it is possible today to describe technical dependencies and requirements early enough, the impact on a service provider's total business effectiveness and efficiency can only be insufficiently calculated due to the missing computational cost instruments.

4.2.2 Integrated Cost Tables as Calculation Instruments

In order to avoid the described deficits of today's calculation procedures, a new approach to the integrated calculation of IT products should exhibit the following characteristics:

- It should stipulate *the use of a customer oriented, consistent service definition,* which is valid for both development and production.
- It should *focus more on the phase of product planning* because in the context of planning a majority of the subsequent production costs is defined (see Chapter 2.4).
- It should create an *integrated development and production cost perspective.*
- It should have the capability of an economical and practical implementation.

A cost table is an instrument which, to a great extent, fulfills these requirements. Today they are used for the most part in the Japanese manufacturing industry and serve in estimating and planning product costs. In a cost table different service development and production alternatives are compared with respect to costs. In the context of an IT service provider's cost calculation, they can thus be used as instruments for supporting decision-making.

For the realization of an IT service, usually different development and production alternatives exist. For example, a service can be realized with the help of a monolithic application, which contains all necessary functions, or by organizing a modular architecture consisting of several individual application modules. Different development alternatives are also usually available for the use and organization of standard solutions. As an example, the IT service "Email Service" can be developed either on the basis of a Microsoft Exchange platform or a Lotus Notes platform.

Just as there are different alternatives for the development of an IT service, so there are for the production of an IT service. As a function of the requirements, in particular customer-defined quantities, various possibilities for the organization of production infrastructure exist. Thus, various server platforms, storage concepts, or network topologies can be implemented. Henceforth these alternatives are referred to as production alternatives.

The choice of a development alternative will exclude certain production alternatives. For example, if the above-mentioned IT service "Email Service" is built based on a Microsoft Exchange solution, then Unix servers are no longer possible alternatives for production. Nevertheless, despite these restrictions there are usually different production alternatives for each development alternative, because production systems can differ with regard to different aspects, for instance, their scalability or availability.

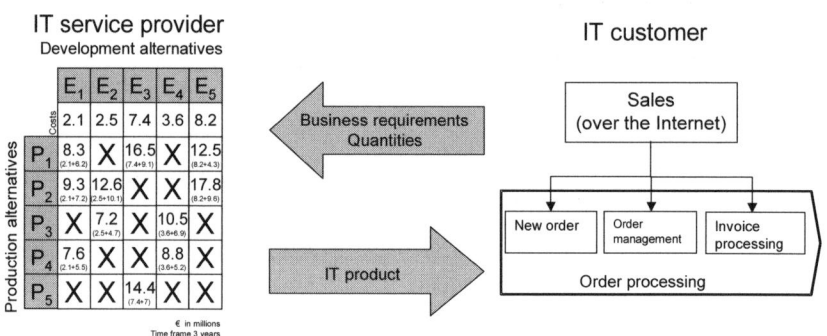

Fig. 61. Matrix of development and production alternatives

The creation of an integrated cost table is performed in several steps. The following example demonstrates the process (see Fig. 61):

- *Step 1 – Specification of technical requirements and quantities*: A customer would like to buy for its business process "Internet Sales" an IT product which supports order processing. This IT product should provide support for new orders, order management, and invoice processing. In a first step the customer must specify the business, i.e. functional requirements demanded of the IT product. Furthermore, quantity structures must be estimated (e.g. forecasted number of executed processes per year). Quantity structures strongly influence the possible choices of technical implementation and consequently product costs. A product which must process 20 Internet-based orders daily must be constructed differently than a solution that must process 20 000 orders daily. The better the quantity structures match the actual quantity required, the smaller the risk of the solution having incorrect dimensions; this is significant with regard to production.

- *Step 2 – Definition of development alternatives*: The service provider can derive and specify possible development alternatives based on business requirements and quantities. In the context of specification, the different alternatives should be described with respect to, for example, the architecture (the type and number of modules, the organization of functionality and data storage, the type and number of interfaces), the user interface, the use of standard solutions or the required operating system. Although the specification of several development alternatives is costly in the planning phase, this can be justified with a holistic view of the product life cycle. The justification is as follows: The majority of a product's later life cycle costs originate in the specification definitions. However, the goal is not to specify as large a number of theoretical development alternatives as possible, but instead a manageable number of realistic alternatives. In order to estimate the feasibility of a development alternative, it can be helpful to develop experimental prototypes already in the context of the specification.

- *Step 3 – Cost estimation of development alternatives*: After the development alternatives are derived from the technical requirements and system oriented specifications described, the costs of the alternatives must be estimated in a third step. The previously mentioned various expenditure and cost estimation procedures used in development are applicable here again. The estimated costs of development alternatives are presented in the horizontal axis of the cost table.

- *Step 4 – Estimation of required quantities in production*: The subsequent production costs of an IT product are strongly correlated to the definition of technical parameters in development. Thus, every development alternative possesses specific characteristics regarding its production resource requirements. Whereas one development alternative, for instance, would permit production resources to be used very efficiently, another alternative can lead to a much greater production resource expenditure, relatively speaking. Therefore it is of utmost importance to estimate already in the planning phase the expected quantities of production resources required for each development alternative. This is common practice in industrial manufacturing and is implemented using production parts list in work scheduling. However, it is largely unknown within the realm of IT. Thus, in order to create an analogous procedure, IT parts lists must specify which production resources the production of an IT product will require and in what quantities. In IT the three basic services "Processing," "Memory" and "Transmission" can be considered cornerstones for part differentiation. A parts list must be prepared for each development alternative. This parts list must indicate what quantities of each of the IT basic services the actual production of an IT product will require (see Fig. 62).

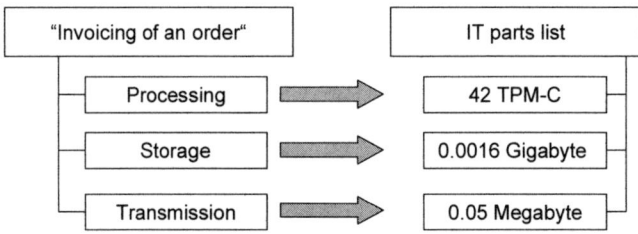

Fig. 62. IT product "Invoice Processing" parts list

Concrete required quantity forecasts can be based on past observations or with the help of known estimation techniques. Using past observations is an especially viable method when considering existing IT products, for example basing requirements on past production performance and utilization data. The methods of Software Performance Engineering (SPE) can be drawn upon for a completely new product, for which there exists no observational data. SPE allows for forecasting application system performance and resource utilization in the development stage [Dumke et al. 2001].

- *Step 5 – Definition of production alternatives*: Analogous to the development procedure, possible production alternatives for an IT product must be specified. These result particularly from the actual design and organization of parameters such as hardware (e.g. platform, type of processor, number of processors), system software (e.g. operating system and data base management system), storage media (type, number, size), scalability, and availability.

- *Step 6 – Cost estimation of production alternatives*: The costs of a production alternative are essentially hardware, software, and personnel expenditures. There are diverse other costs to be added in, for example for rent or electricity. Production costs depend on the development alternative because each development alternative has a unique resource expenditure set. Two development alternatives can differ, for example, in their requirement of computing power, which in turn leads to different requirements for hardware and thus also to different production costs. Concrete production costs can be forecasted based on the parts list and the required product quantity, because with this information necessary quantities or levels of computing power, memory, and transmission can be calculated. The selection and dimensioning of the production alternatives is based on these expenditure quantities or levels. Beyond that, the production time line must also be considered. Although development costs are independent of their life span, production costs do, indeed, depend on it. The total costs for each production alternative as a function of the development alternative form the vertical axis of the cost table.

- *Step 7 – Determining total costs*: By adding together development and production costs, the total costs for each alternative combination can be calculated (see Fig. 63). Like production costs, the total costs are presented for a defined time span. A unit cost calculation of an IT product is possible, given that the total costs are divided by the number of required products.

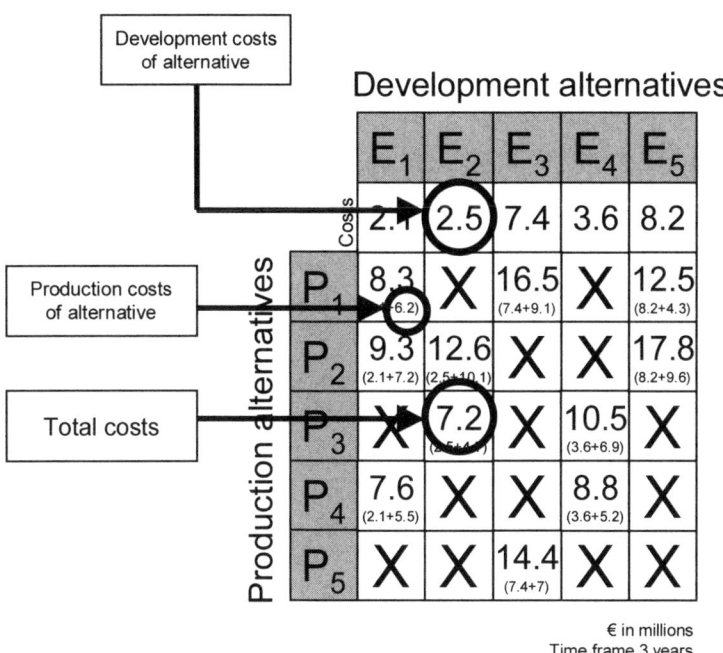

Fig. 63. Integrated IT cost table

In the example illustrated in Fig. 63, it is apparent that—considering only cost criteria—the combination of the development alternative E2 and the production alternative P3 presents the best solution for the 3-year time frame with total costs reaching € 7.2 million. However, this does not necessarily mean that this combination will inevitably be implemented. Another combination may, for example, be more expensive but possess better upward scalability characteristics. If there is a likelihood that the service provider may sell this product to other customers, which would lead to greater production quantities, then this other alternative combination could be better despite the higher base costs.

All in all, an integrated IT cost table supplies the service provider with a comprehensive, life cycle, and product oriented cost calculation. It can be used as a basis for comparing different development and production alternatives, and also as a starting point for price calculations and negotiations with customers.

4.2.3 Prototyping Selected Elements

A prototype based on SAP was made to demonstrate a central component of the presented solution concept. The prototype permits:

- the definition and specification of different production alternatives for an IT product (Step 5) and·
- the cost-related evaluation of production alternatives for a given development alternative (Step 6)

The prototype gives an IT service provider's product manager an instrument, which enables him to calculate production costs of a product based on a specific development alternative and this for different production alternatives. In this calculation also idle capacities on servers already employed are taken into account. The prototype is introduced in the following example.

A service provider would like to calculate costs for the IT product "Internet Sales." The customer's functional requirements on the product are well defined. Two different development alternatives were specified for the product. Now, for each development alternative, expected production costs are to be calculated, taking into account the existing production infrastructure.

Ressource	Hersteller	Ressourcenbeschreibung	Prozessor-Typ	Prozessor	OS
1	Fujitsu Siemens	PRIMERGY R450	Intel Xeon MP 2.00 GHz	4	Microsoft Windows Server 2003 Enterprise Edition
2	Fujitsu Siemens	PRIMERGY T850	Intel MP 1.6GHz	8	Microsoft Windows Server 2003 Enterprise Edition
3	Fujitsu Siemens	PRIMERGY R450	Intel Xeon MP 1.6GHz	4	Microsoft Windows 2000 Advanced Server
4	Fujitsu Siemens	PRIMERGY H250	Intel Xeon 2.20 GHz	2	Microsoft Windows 2000 Advanced Server
5	Fujitsu Siemens	Primergy F200	Intel Pentium III 1266 MHz	2	Microsoft Windows 2000 Server SP2
6	Fujitsu Siemens	PRIMERGY H400 C/S with 3 PRIMERG	Intel Pentium III Xeon 900 MHz	4	Microsoft Windows 2000

Ressource	Hersteller	Ressourcenbeschreibung	Prozessor-Typ	Prozessor	OS
1	HP	HP 9000 Model Superdome Enterprise S	HP PA-RISC 8700 875MHz	64	HP UX 11.i 64-bit
2	HP	HP 9000 Superdome Enterprise Server	HP PA-RISC 8700 750MHz	64	HP UX 11.i 64-bit
3	HP	hp server rp8400	HP PA-RISC 8700 750MHz	16	HP UX 11.i 64-bit

Ressource	Hersteller	Ressourcenbeschreibung	Prozessor-Typ	Prozessor	OS
1	IBM	IBM eServer pSeries 690 Model 7040-68	IBM POWER4+ 1.9GHz	32	IBM AIX 5L V5.2
2	IBM	IBM eServer pSeries 690 Turbo 7040-681	IBM Power 4 1700 MHz	32	IBM AIX 5L V5.2
3	IBM	IBM eServer pSeries 690 Turbo 7040-681	IBM Power 4 1700 MHz	32	IBM AIX 5L V5.2
4	IBM	IBM eServer pSeries 690 Turbo 7040-681	IBM Power 4 1700 MHz	32	IBM AIX 5L V5.2
5	IBM	IBM eServer pSeries 660 Model 6M1	IBM RS64 IV 750MHz	8	IBM AIX 4.3.3
6	IBM	IBM eServer pSeries 680 Model 7017-S8	IBM RS64 IV 600 MHz	24	IBM AIX 4.3.3
7	IBM	IBM eServer pSeries 660	IBM RS64 IV 668 MHz	6	IBM AIX 4.3.3

Fig. 64. All possible production resources for a development alternative: an overview

The specification of the development Alternative 1 allows for a production on hardware resources presented in Fig. 64. Each resource must be described in detail with respect to its technical and economical information in the system. Fig. 65 presents an example of this for the technical information of a server. The fundamental data as to the type of server, CPU size, CPU type, operating system type and version are described foremost. The server provides two types of computing measurements, "storage capacity," measured in gigabytes, and "processing capacity," measured in TPM-C (Transactions Per Minute-C). For each computing measurement, the maximal capacity (CAP_SLAM) can be specified. The so-called k-point (KPP_SLAM), i.e. the extent of utilization from which, in practice, a decline in server performance must be reckoned with, and the planned capacity (PLM_SLAM), also known as the planned utilization, can be specified.

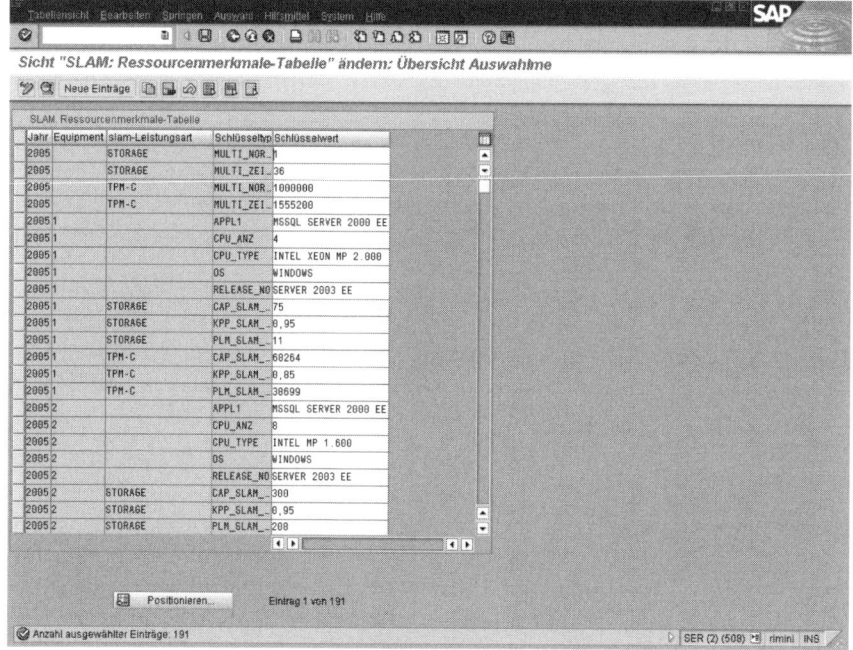

Fig. 65. Technical resource characteristics of a server

In this illustration the economic descriptions of the server, which must be entered, are not shown. These include financial dimensions, for example purchase price and annual amortization. Also those cost categories of production which are recorded in SAP-CO must be either directly assigned to the computing services "Processing" and "Storage" or allocated using some kind of distribution key. Exactly for this purpose, it is possible to define permanent allocation keys in this system.

With this the prerequisites for product calculation are fulfilled. The business information from SAP-CO, that is cost category and cost center accounting, as well as all technical resource information are joined together in the system. A Product Configurator is the core of the system. It combines this information according to predefined criteria. Fig. 66 presents the functionality of the Product Configurator using the example of the product "Internet Sales Support." The plan is to make the product available starting in year 2005 with an assumed service life of 3 years. In order to fulfill customer requirements, development Alternative 1 stipulates a capacity requirement of 245 000 TPM-C. For the 3-year period of use, the total requirement amounts to 25.2 million standardized transactions. Similarly the time-relevant requirement for storage capacity is 2.5 GB, the total requirement is 1620 GB months. Qualitative requirements of the product, for example regarding the operating system, the data base management system, or the type of processor, can be specified in a similar fashion.

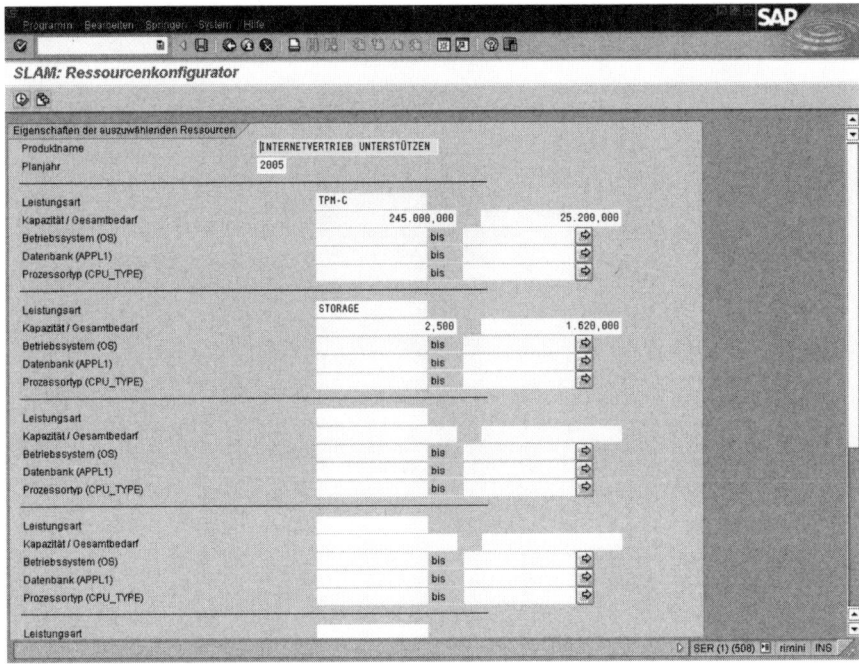

Fig. 66. IT Product Configurator

With this information, the Product Configurator can compute production costs on all possible hardware combinations (see Fig. 67). Both qualitative and quantitative requirements are taken into account. Each possible resource combination is expressed as an alternative. The production costs for each resource and each computing service are presented based on the different capacities: first the costs with maximum utilization, then the costs with a utilization of up to the k-point and/or for planned capacity utilization. The next to last column shows the total costs of computing service types.

It is easily seen from the example that in Alternative 7 the two technical computing services TMP-C and STORAGE can be delivered from a technical resource, i.e. Model Group 1 (IT Platform 1) Resource 7 (Computer 1). Here the production of the product "Internet Sales Support" results in costs of approx. € 135 376, providing for the HK max. cap. value, and/or approx. € 151 140 providing for the HK k-point value and approx. € 500 948 for the HK planned capacity value.

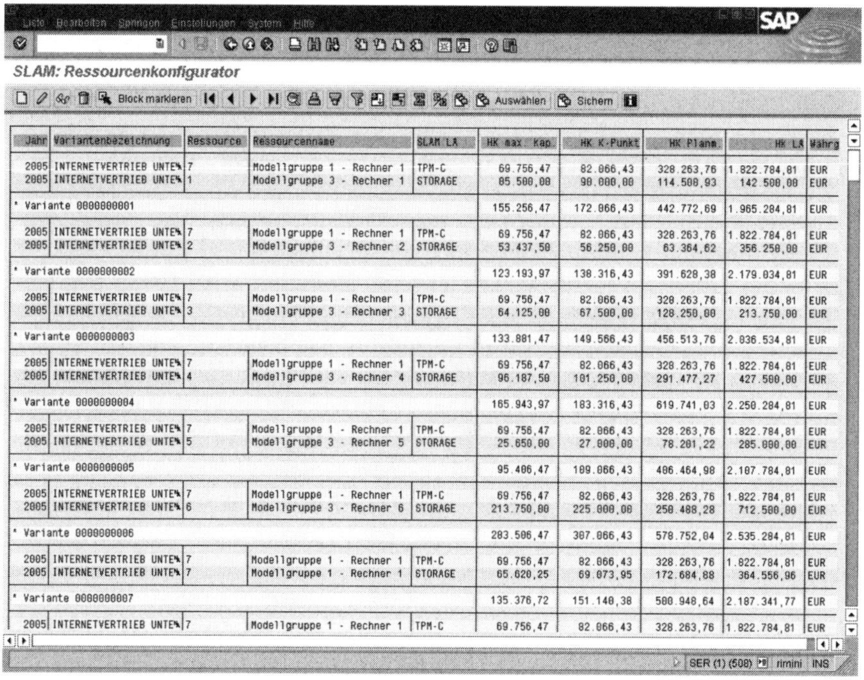

Fig. 67. An overview of production costs

4.3 IT Applications Life Cycle Costs[3]

With the analysis of their cost structures, many IT units observe that investments in new IT projects present a consistently declining share of total IT costs. Thus, for example, at the Deutsche Bank in 2002 new projects accounted for only 27% of total IT costs [Lamberti 2002]. 73% of its IT budget was spent on current production (operating, maintenance, and support) and the enhancement of existing IT solutions. Example 9 is based on further investigations and studies, and substantiates the fact that the Deutsche Bank is not an exception and that its cost allocations are typical.

> **Ex. 9.** Studies on the allocation of IT budgets
>
> Studies and investigations exist, which examine how IT budgets are distributed among the core tasks of information management. Thus, a survey of insurance companies in German-speaking countries led to the following result: in the period 2000/2001 on average 55% of IT expenditure went to compulsory tasks (operating and maintenance of existing infrastructures), 35% to optional tasks (new IT projects), and 10% to planning, controlling, and administration [Jahn et al. 2002]. The Boston Consulting Group gives the typical IT cost allocation with 50–60% to operating costs, 30–40% to application development costs (new and enhancement), and 10% to costs of sovereignty functions (e.g. controlling, architecture) [Thiel 2002]. A study carried out by the consulting company Cap Gemini Ernst & Young on IT trends 2003 stated that most IT expenditures are already fixed by decisions made in the past and only about 30% of the budget is available for new concepts [Cap Gemini Ernst & Young 2003]. About 20% of the survey participants have less than 10% leeway in this area.

The fundamental relationship between the costs of non-recurring project planning and initial development of new IT solutions and recurring costs of production and maintenance of existing solutions is well known. It is addressed by concepts such as Total Cost of Ownership or Life Cycle Costing. Even though the relationship is well known and addressed, in practice in the analysis and evaluation of IT application systems, it often plays only a subordinate role. Thus, for example, the evaluation and prioritization of application systems costs is based primarily on the costs of the development project. Production costs are regarded as only proportional surcharges and, as such, contribute, if at all, to efficiency perspectives. Information about the real scope of an application system's production costs is rarely

---

[3] The information presented in this chapter is based on the collective research of the authors and Jochen Scheeg (see Zarnekow et al. 2004)

systematically reported and evaluated, so that a service provider's knowledge of these costs is limited. Our experience from many discussions with IT management shows that there is an intuitive awareness of the importance of current production costs. However, management has little to no knowledge of its own application system costs over life cycle models, nor has it any concrete numbers or facts regarding life cycle costs.

These issues are mirrored in cost planning procedures. Despite the existence of many methods and tools for planning the costs of software development, often in practice the planning of production costs is left to rough estimation techniques or simple rules of thumb (e.g. a 20:80 rule).

In order to determine the actual composition of application system life cycle costs, we examined 30 application systems with three of our Competence Center partner companies. Interviews and workshops were conducted with application project and system managers, as well as information process controlling (IV Controlling). With the help of a structured collection list based on a standardized life cycle model, the actual life cycle costs were deciphered together with the participants. The subsequent analysis concentrated particularly on the application systems total cost distribution as to the application life cycle phases and on the degree of cost transparency.

4.3.1 The IT Application Life Cycle

Application systems go through a life cycle (see Chapter 2.5). In Fig. 68 the core phases are presented in chronological order. The life cycle of a new application system begins with a planning and an initial development phase. Thereby, in addition to the actual development, the initial development covers integration and testing. At the end of the initial development, the application system is taken into production. Production is the actual operation of the application system, application support (above all user support), and the continuous maintenance of the application system. Parallel to production, application system enhancements are made. In contrast to maintenance, which concentrates particularly on the elimination of errors, enhancements implement new customer requirements and extend functionality. The last phase of the IT application life cycle is the system's retirement.

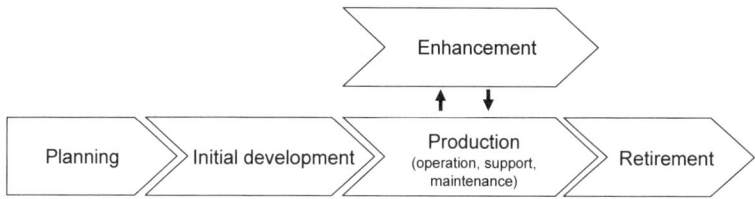

Fig. 68. The life cycle phases of an IT application system

Concrete tasks can be assigned to each life cycle phase. An overview is presented in Fig. 69. Just looking at the tasks, it seems apparent that information management life cycle concepts used in practice today focus mainly on managing the software development life cycle. They thus only partially deal with the phases and tasks presented in the figure below. It is uncommon to work with models which cover entire life cycles; if, then in the form of TCO analyses in the evaluation of workplace systems, hardware platforms, or the employment of system software.

Life Cycle Phase	Task
Planning	Project planning Rough concept Prototype (development, test, evaluation)
Initial development	Business concept / DP concept System design System development (coding) Integration Test Installation / introduction
Production	Training Running operation Corrective maintenance User support
Enhancement	Business concept / DP concept System design System development (coding) Integration Test Installation / introduction
Retirement	Disposal of physical components Secure data for subsequent use Data migration

Fig. 69. Tasks within IT application systems life cycle phases

4.3.2 Life Cycle Cost Analysis

For the analysis of the actual life cycle costs of application systems, 30 application systems from three partner companies were examined. The investigated application systems were of various magnitudes, as well as having different core business and support processes. Both internally developed and standard software solutions were represented. With regard to the technical architecture, both batch and online application systems, as well as host and client/server-based solutions were represented.

Actual costs imposed by an application system formed the basis for the computation. In order to guarantee a comparability of cost information, the life cycle model presented in the previous section was given as the framework in cost collection. Using a structured collection list, the actual costs involved in each task actual were deciphered together with the respective company's application project managers and system managers. Actual application costs were defined as all those costs directly resulting from hardware, software, and personnel expenditures. As much as possible, costs of reusable infrastructure components (e.g. middleware or databases) were assigned proportionately to the application systems.

Status: June 2003	Times (in years)			Actual costs (in Mio. €)					
	Total age	Initial development	Production	Total costs	Planning	Initial development	Enhancement	Production	Retirement
Application 1	16.4	3.0	12.4	-	-	-	-	-	-
Application 2	9.3	1.8	5.9	-	-	3.30	25.40	-	-
Application 3	3.4	1.8	0.8	-	-	14.00	4.90	5.48	-
Application 4	7.2	2.0	3.9	137.33	1.80	24.71	2.72	108.10	-
Application 5	7.4	-	4.8	-	-	85.00	38.00	117.80	-
Application 6	2.4	1.6	0.6	63.99	2.07	30.00	24.10	7.82	-
Application 7	8.3	2.9	3.4	-	-	2.30	2.96	1.57	-
Application 8	3.3	1.0	0.8	2.96	0.13	2.08	0.00	0.75	-
Application 9	3.2	0.3	1.8	3.44	0.36	0.41	1.30	1.37	-
Application 10	8.4	2.9	3.4	31.20	2.40	13.00	3.50	12.30	-
Application 11	4.9	2.9	0.4	-	0.20	0.90	-	-	-
Application 12	9.4	1.3	4.2	19.35	0.70	0.55	2.50	15.60	-
Application 13	2.0	2.0	-	-	1.64	-	-	-	-
Application 14	9.4	3.0	3.9	-	-	13.00	-	-	-
Application 15	2.8	2.1	-	-	2.60	19.21	1.02	-	0.00
Application 16	4.0	0.8	2.5	-	-	0.58	0.39	0.20	-
Application 17	11.4	2.9	6.3	-	50.00	80.00	-	52.08	-
Application 18	3.1	0.6	2.2	16.33	0.39	1.02	9.50	5.42	-
Application 19	2.9	2.0	0.9	4.86	0.10	1.37	0.00	3.39	-
Application 20	3.3	0.8	1.4	5.49	0.72	1.96	0.50	2.31	-
Application 21	3.4	0.4	2.4	0.64	0.13	0.21	0.12	0.18	-
Application 22	5.8	0.3	4.8	0.90	0.01	0.19	0.06	0.64	-
Application 23	7.3	2.3	3.7	3.36	0.27	1.13	0.67	1.22	0.07
Application 24	2.9	0.9	1.4	0.50	0.13	0.13	0.10	0.14	-
Application 25	5.3	1.0	2.4	1.87	0.11	0.64	0.32	0.80	-
Application 26	2.4	0.9	-	-	3.00	-	-	-	-
Application 27	6.4	1.9	2.5	8.09	1.07	1.07	2.67	3.15	0.13
Application 28	5.0	2.9	-	-	0.20	6.00	-	-	-
Application 29	3.8	0.8	2.4	-	0.10	2.40	-	0.71	-
Application 30	3.3	1.0	0.8	9.56	0.29	7.20	0.67	1.30	0.10
Minimum	2.0	0.3	0.4	0.50	0.01	0.13	0.00	0.14	0.00
Maximum	16.4	3.0	12.4	137.33	50.00	85.00	38.00	117.80	0.13
Average	5.6	1.7	3.1	19.37	2.97	11.57	5.52	15.56	0.08

Fig. 70. Age and actual costs of the examined application systems

In Fig. 70 the critical data of age and actual costs of each of the examined application systems is presented in total and with respect to its life cycle phases. The total age of the application systems lies between 2 and 16.4 years; the average is 5.6 years. The total age begins with the beginning of planning and ends with retirement, and/or application systems in production up to the time of the investigation. The age is essentially determined by the production duration. Of course this is apparent in our sample, where the youngest applications had the minimum production duration of 0.4 years, and oldest application systems a maximum production duration of 12.4 years. The average production duration is 3.1 years. The total costs of the application systems lie between € 0.5 million and € 137.33 million. In most cases retirement costs were unknown because at the time of this investigation the application systems were still in production.

The cost information listed as both current and absolute in Fig. 70 is somewhat misleading for the proportional allocation of entire life cycle costs to the individual phase costs. These costs strongly depend on the different ages of the application systems. For application systems taken into production only recently, the relative share of the initial development costs of total costs is very high. In this case there has been little time to incur production and enhancement costs. Conversely, old application systems, having been in production for longer periods, carry accordingly high shares of total life cycle costs in their production phases. The final cost allocation can only be correctly made when the application is removed from production, i.e. at the end of the application life cycle. Since most of the examined application systems were still in production at the time of this investigation, this was not possible. Instead, for the following discussion life cycle costs were generated, assuming a production duration of 5 years. In order to generate these figures, the costs of the application systems were extrapolated based on the given cost information.

The planning and initial development costs are singular one-time expenditures. They are independent of the total life duration. The costs of production and enhancement increase as total life duration increases. For this reason the generated figures for the assumed 5-year total production duration had to be either marked up or discounted. The result of this standardization of the application systems' total production duration was that the figures were now comparable with respect to their cost structures. The extrapolation was made under the assumption of a uniform distribution of enhancement and production costs within the duration of production. Although, in reality, this is not entirely accurate, in particular with respect to enhancement costs, the investigation data analysis shows that this assumption causes no substantial changes in the test results. Principally, however, it should be noted that enhancement and production costs usually rise with increasing production duration.

Fig. 71 presents the percentage of costs allocated over the life cycle with a total production duration of 5 years. Sixteen application systems are taken into consideration. The only systems considered are those for which actual cost information was able to be completely identified. With a total production duration of 5 years, on the average recurring costs make up 79% of total costs. In practice, the definite average total production duration of application systems, however, is probably greater than these 5 years, and thus this percentage is probably higher. In the analysis of cost distributions, there are obvious differences and high fluctuations between the individual application systems. The share of singular, one-time planning, and initial development costs lies between a minimum of 4% and a maximum of 40%. Although different factors are responsible for this great variation, one aspect was particularly conspicuous. In application systems having percentage-wise low singular, one-time costs, the enhancement costs are very high compared with the initial development costs (this applies for example to the application systems 6, 9, 12, 18, and 27). A more exact data analysis and discussions with the application owners leads to the following conclusion. These application systems, due to intense time pressure or delays in the project scheduling, were put in production before the initial development work was completed or without sufficient testing. Development work and error elimination, which are actually a part of initial development, therefore were realized only after start-up of the application system and this in turn increased the costs of enhancement and production.

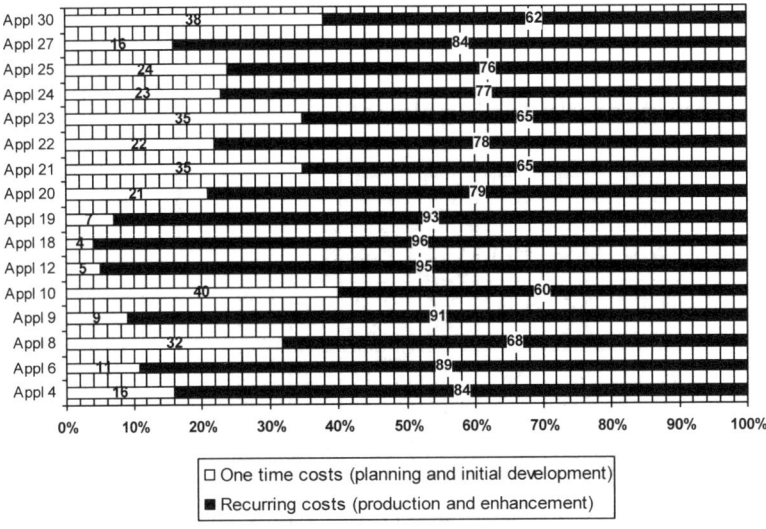

Fig. 71. Cost distribution with an assumed total production duration of 5 years

The quality of the data collected added to further understanding. Insight was gained from precise fundamental information about the functionality, purpose, and supported processes of the application systems, as well as user numbers and temporal information regarding planning, development, and production duration. Additionally, usually information about the type and number of business transactions was available. A completely different picture was presented with respect to cost information. The analysis of the captured data demonstrated that cost information was usually only able to be reconstructed with many gaps and assumptions. A life cycle perspective of application systems did not exist in the companies involved. A phase spanning cost controlling was atypical. The costs of the initial development could be assessed most accurately because these costs had been documented both in the context of project development and project controlling. Production costs were for the most part unplanned and were even partially unknown. This caused these costs to be poorly documented, and they were only able to be reconstructed with much time and effort. Since there were no consistent and documented cost perspectives, the quality of data was highly dependent on the application owners' personal knowledge of the application system. Problems arose particularly with older applications, for which over the course of time different persons were responsible, or with very complex application systems, for which several persons were responsible. With about half of the evaluated application systems, the cost information was so incomplete that it did not allow for an analysis of the life cycle costs. Application owners were astonished at the presentation of the test results, which demonstrated how their initial estimations differed from the actual cost allocations over life cycles.

4.3.3 Consequences for Information Management

From the insight gained, several conclusions can be made. The critical impact of production and enhancement costs on total costs of application systems, and thereby on IT costs overall, is not sufficiently reflected in the information management instruments used in practice. Instead development is strongly focused and zeroed in on. In order to prevent wrong business decisions, life cycle oriented cost calculation models for application systems must be developed and implemented. Today, in practice, attempts fail due to fundamental problems, such as using one cost object for development and a different one for production (see Chapter 4.2).

A life cycle perspective is suitable for both the analysis of new application systems and the management of existing application systems. For new application systems, this perspective facilitates a more qualified decision as to the total expected costs. The augmentation of widely used IT project portfolios, which in their current form serve above all in prioritizing development projects, to life cycle oriented IT product portfolios is a first step in this direction (see Fig. 72). Using a life cycle perspective for existing application systems facilitates better management decisions, for example in determining the most cost-effective point in time for retiring an application system. Today this decision is made, if at all, on the basis of technical considerations or ad hoc decisions and not in the context of an institutionalized management process.

The prerequisite for a life cycle cost calculation is the collection and recording of application-system-related actual costs. This entails developing procedures and tools, which allow for a collective application system bookkeeping in the sense of an asset accounting. Application system bookkeeping will be of utmost importance, at the latest when implementing balance regulations, for example IAS (International Accounting Standards). These new regulations call for the inclusion of software as assets in the balance sheet. Furthermore, it leads to a significant improvement of cost transparency for all concerned and provides business units as well as IT service providers with a complete real time overview of application-system-related costs.

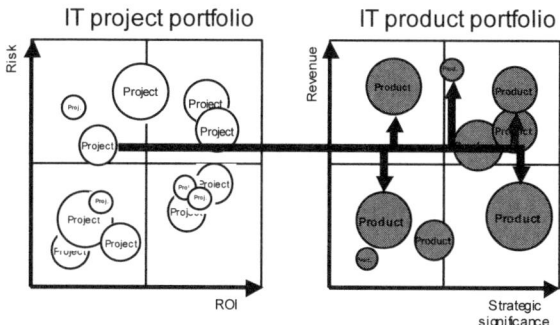

Planning object	Project, application	Product
Planning basis	Project costs (primarily costs of development)	Product life cycle (development and production), unit costs

Fig. 72. From an IT project to an IT product portfolio

Life cycle perspectives promote the development of holistic, integrated information management approaches. In the examination of life cycle costs, it became evident that management approaches implemented in practice today exhibit a strong phase orientation. They are optimized for individual phases, for example Planning, Development, or Production. Phase-spanning approaches, as required in the context of a life cycle perspective or as, for example, found in industrial product manufacturing, are seldom seen in the IT business area.

Last but not least, statistically substantiated facts on the actual division of application system life cycle costs are missing. The investigation results presented in this chapter can demonstrate, due to its small database, only an initial step in this direction. For more general statements further, more extensive investigations and a focus on special application segments are necessary.

4.4 IT Product Value Analysis

Today, in manufacturing as well as in service industries, value analysis is generally acknowledged as a universal procedure for solving complex problems [Zentrum Wertanalyse 1995]. It is considered fundamental to rationalization. In the last 25 years it has been regarded as one of the most important methods of cost reduction. It is all the more surprising that, in practice, up until now value analysis has played a negligible role in the definition and improvement of IT products. The following example demonstrates how, in the context of integrated information management, value analysis can be used for the requirement analysis and specification of IT products. This example also demonstrates the potential benefit implementing value analysis presents for the IT service provider. Some principles and fundamental concepts of value analysis are described first.

4.4.1 Principles and Fundamental Concepts of Value Analysis

According to Larry Miles, the founder of value analysis, it is a methodical procedure to provide product functions at the lowest possible costs without negatively affecting the demanded quality, reliability, and marketability of the product [Miles 1972]. Already in 1947 as Head of Purchasing at General Electrics, Miles made a surprising discovery; in searching for alternative materials or procedures for the production of a product, frequently lower cost solutions were found enabling identical, if not sometimes even better, product functionality. Not only this, he also found that a significant share of production costs is spent on the production of product functions, which are of little or no use to customers.

In light of this, Miles developed a systematic procedure under the heading "value analysis" with the goal of:

- identifying the *functions* of a product or a service
- assigning the functions a monetary *value*
- manufacturing product functions at the required level of quality at the lowest *total costs*

Two central principles shape value analysis. The first is thinking in functions instead of products. The other is thinking in values instead of costs. The functions of a product are its characteristics, so that it functions and can be sold. Typical characteristics of a product can be, for example, properties, elements, conditions, components, or specialties. They result from the question: "What does the product do?" A function of a clock is for example "indicate time," the function of a train "to transport people from one place to another." The appearance of a product is also a function, for example the sporty appearance of a car. There are different types of functions. Especially, of practical importance is the distinction between main, secondary, and unnecessary functions. The respective function type can be categorized with the help of simple questions (see Fig. 73). When thinking in functions, it is necessary to analyze and describe the characteristics of a product in an output oriented manner, and thus with a customer orientation. Technical characteristics (e.g. the application systems, server platforms, networks, or architectures), which are necessary for the production of an IT product, are not at the center of a product definition, but instead the functions the customer recognizes in the product. Also, in the context of value analysis, the costs of a product are assigned exclusively to its functions and not to its technical product components.

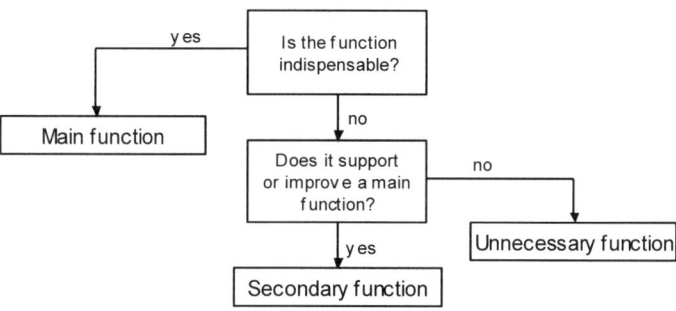

Fig. 73. Function type identification

As well as thinking in terms of functions, in value analysis thinking in terms of values plays a central role. Value analysis is based on cost oriented value concepts. The value of a product corresponds to the lowest costs which must be spent so that the product provides the defined functions reliably. A consequence of this way of thinking is that neither the cheapest nor the most expensive product is the most valuable. Thus, for example, neither the cheapest nor the most expensive printer is of most value, but instead that printer which provides the demanded function, for example "to print presentations," in the demanded quality, or "color print at a speed of four pages per minute," at the lowest cost per page. Additionally, value analysis focuses on the key question: which element of the total cost of a product actually generates its value? All expenditures which do not contribute to its value represent unnecessary costs and are to be eliminated. This applies especially to costs incurred in the production of unnecessary functions.

This value and function paradigm is what distinguishes value analysis from pure rationalization measures, which concentrate particularly on product and cost characteristics. If, for example, an IT service provider realizes that its product "Desktop Service" is too expensive, then rationalization measures would typically pose questions such as: Can the costs of the product be decreased? Can the product be designed or structured in a cheaper way? Can the individual elements of the product be produced less expensively or bought at a lower price?, etc. [Hoffmann 1994]. In contrast, in a value analysis framework the questions posed would look like: What product functions are actually required? What functions can we do without and what new functions do we need? What monetary value do the functions possess? What production costs contribute to the value of this product? If a function of the IT product "Desktop Service" is, for example, "Send Email," then the question posed under value analysis is to the value of this function. This value corresponds to the minimum costs necessary for the function "Send Email," whereby a differentiation can certainly be made in the levels of quality. Thus, for example, customer requirements for sending encrypted emails, storing emails for a longer period of time, or examining emails for viruses will result in different cost levels and thus have different values.

A value analysis is carried out in a project framework. Procedure methodology is strictly systematic and is divided into several phases (see Fig. 74). In the information phase all available information about the product under examination is collected. This information can come from different business units, for example marketing, production, development, purchasing, or finance. Especially for existing products, which should be improved in the context of a value analysis, a multitude of diverse information can usually be found. An actual state analysis is carried out based on this collected information. Here the two central questions are:

- *What does the product do?* That is, what functions does it provide?
- *What do the functions cost?*

To answer both questions, value analysis presents concrete instruments, for example function analysis trees and function cost matrices.

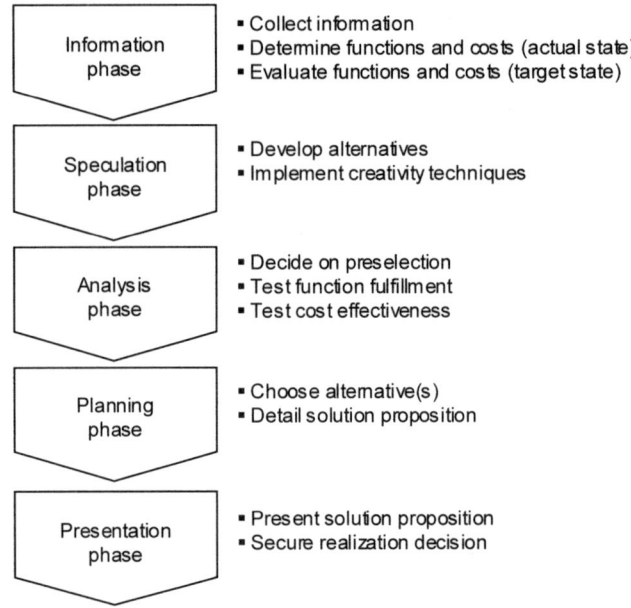

Fig. 74. Procedural systematic and phases of value analysis

After the actual analysis, the actual state is examined and evaluated. Here the question posed, for example, is whether or not all of the current product functions are of importance or whether some functions can be eliminated. The result of this analysis is a target group of functions. The same applies to function costs, which are to be analyzed in a similar fashion. Here, above all, the central cost drivers should be identified, i.e. those functions which incur most costs. These costs are usually a good starting point for further analysis.

The speculation phase is the second phase of value analysis. The primary goal of speculation is to obtain as large a number of alternatives as possible. All of the alternatives should include product functions at the demanded level of reliability. Alternatives can result from, for example, using different technologies, structures, components, or production procedures. In developing alternatives, value analysis proposes the use of various creativity techniques, for example brainstorming, synectics, or morphologic analysis.

The alternatives are judged and evaluated in the analysis phase. Usually at the beginning of the analysis phase a preselection is met, so that the number of alternatives is manageable. These alternatives are then refined and specified accordingly. In particular, the degree of function fulfillment and cost effectiveness are investigated.

In the planning phase a precise solution proposal is formulated based on the selected alternative. In the following presentation phase, this proposal will be presented to a decision-making body. The goal of this presentation is to gain permission to actually implement this proposal.

Value analysis is especially suitable for the solution of interdisciplinary and complex problems. In the context of IT product design, value analysis can be used, in particular, for requirement analysis and product specification. It can be used for both the design of completely new IT products and the improvement of existing products. Customer and market oriented specifications for products are a great challenge for many IT service providers. In practice the threat of misunderstandings and conflicts lurk in several corners of the specification process (see Fig. 75).

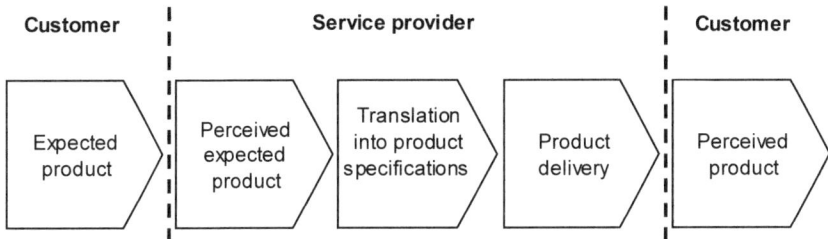

Fig. 75. Perception/expectation: interfaces in product delivery (according to [Zeithaml et al. 1988])

A customer's genuine expectations of a product can deviate from a service provider's perceived customer expectations; the customer understands the product with regard to its business oriented benefit, for example, and the service provider has a technology oriented understanding of the product. The product actually produced then can again deviate from perceived product expectations, for example due to the service provider's internal communication problems between sales and development units. The product specifications and the actual produced product do not always match entirely, maybe because in the context of development or production changes were made or problems arose. And finally there can also be discrepancies between the customer's perception of the product and the actual produced product, because a part of the provided product is not clear to the customer.

This potential conflict can be lessened in two ways with the help of value analysis: Value analysis can contribute to a better match between product specifications and real customer requirements. It can also support the service provider in producing the products expected by the customer at the lowest possible costs.

4.4.2 Value Analysis for the IT Product "Email Service"

The following example shows the process and results of a value analysis for an IT product "Email Service." The numbers given in the example are fictional. The example starts out from the following situation: An internal IT service provider has been providing an email service to the company's business units for several years. For a monthly lump sum each user receives an email account, through which he can send, receive, and manage his emails. The service contains a set of additional services, for example mobile access over a Web interface, a spam filter, and a possibility to save emails over a longer period of time. Most recently the internal service provider has been subject to swelling competition in the product segment "Email." In particular Application Service Providers (ASPs) are bringing increasingly attractive products to the market. The first business units have already evaluated such offers and insist on better product agreements. For this reason the internal service provider decides on performing a value analysis of its "Email Service." The project team is given the following targets:

- 30% reduction of product costs
- Standardization of technical email infrastructure
- Improvement of data security

The value analysis was orchestrated with the procedural systematic and in the project phases described in the previous section.

Phase 1: Information Phase

In a first step all available information about the present "Email Service" is to be collected. This includes both technical documents (e.g. IT concepts, product requirement specifications, system descriptions, architectures, server platforms, etc.) and application quantity structures (e.g. current number of email accounts, storage volumes, transmission volumes, number of sent and received emails, etc).

The actual state was analyzed using the collected information as a base. The first step in the analysis was analysis of functions and the functional hierarchy of the product at hand "Email Service." On the left side of Fig. 78 the main and secondary functions of the product are listed. Complex secondary functions can be subdivided and detailed even further, but for our purpose this level of detail is sufficient. To be able to provide these functions, a production infrastructure is necessary. For the product "Email Service" this includes the components client (above all email client software), server (email server software and hardware), memory (central memory systems), network (LAN and WAN), printer and support (user support, administration). The individual secondary functions can be assigned to the components, as presented in Fig. 76.

In the second step of the actual state analysis, which is based on the function analysis tree, function costs are identified. Initially, the annual costs of individual components of the production infrastructure were established. These include both the actual material costs (e.g. hardware costs or software licenses) and personnel expenditures (e.g. for maintenance, administration, or user support). In order to calculate unit cost, the annual total costs for each component were divided by the number of email accounts. In this way a unit cost was calculated for each account.

For the value analysis the unit costs must be translated into product functions. Since the IT service provider did not have function oriented cost information, the translation to functions was made using an estimated distribution key. A function cost matrix served as a tool, as presented in Fig. 77. On the horizontal axis the components of the infrastructure, their respective annual unit cost prices per component, and email account are listed. Thus, for example, the provision, use, and administration of email servers (including software) incur annual costs of € 178 per email account. Using the previously defined distribution key, these costs were then divided among the individual secondary functions. As a result, the annual costs per function can be identified. Thus the function "Deliver Email" in the illustrated example incurs costs of € 50 per year.

142   Practical Examples of Integrated Information Management

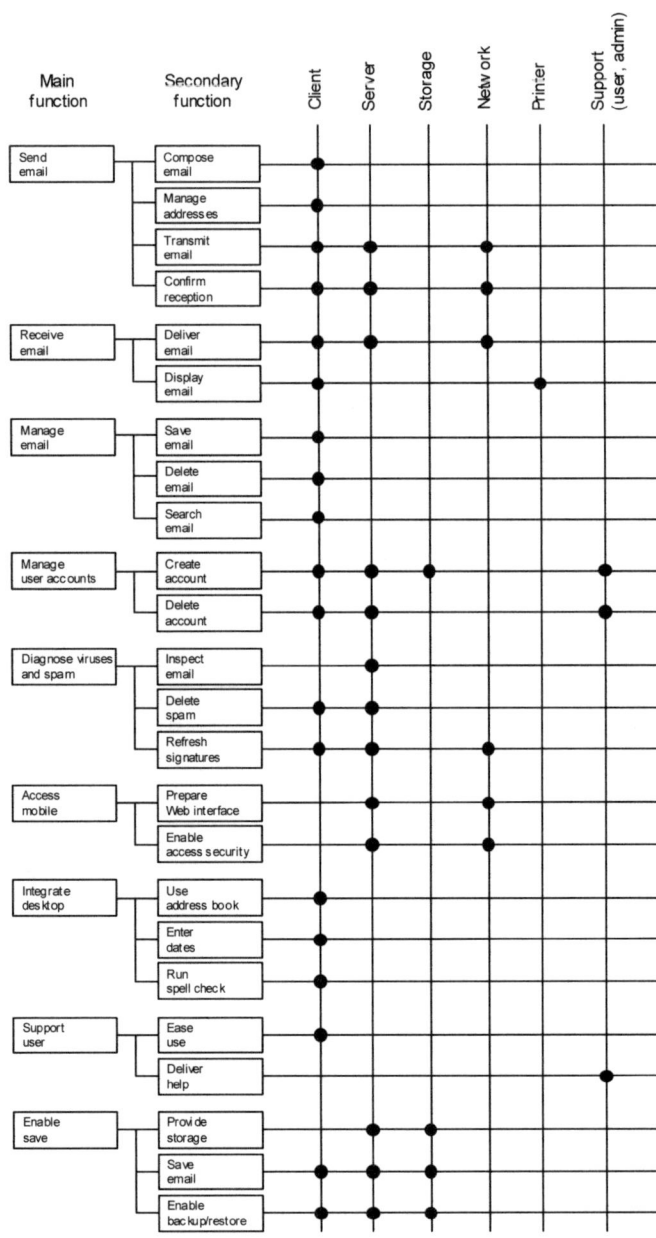

Fig. 76. Actual state function analysis tree and production components

The last step of the information phase is the examination and evaluation of the actual situation. This is done primarily with respect to function fulfillment and costs. An examination of the actual functions showed that users rarely requested the main function "Integrate Desktop." However, the main function "Diagnose Viruses and Spam" should be further developed into a more encompassing function "Ensure Security." In addition to existing functions, above all the secondary functions should facilitate a secure transmission of emails, for example encrypting or signature. In the medium term the main function "Access Mobile" must be further developed in order to access not only the Web interface, but also to support access from other mobile devices such as PDAs or mobile telephones. However, this extension is not of highest priority.

		Components (annual costs per e-mail-account)						
		Client	Server	Memory	Network	Printer	Support	Sum of annual function costs
			178 €					
Send Mail	Write Mail							
	Manage adresses							
	Send Mail		27 €					
	Acknowledge receive		4 €					
Receive Mail	Download Mail	6 €	32 €		12 €			50 €
	Show Mail							
Administrate Mail	Store Mail							
	Delete Mail							
	Search Mail							
Manage Mail accounts	New Account		17 €					
	Delete Account		4 €					
Check for Virus/Spam	Check Mail		15 €					
	Delete Spam		8 €					
	Modify signature		10 €					
Remote access	Provide Web-Interface		26 €					
	Implement Access control		19 €					
Desktop integration	Use adress book							
	Enter meetings							
	Check spelling							
User support	Easy usage							
	Provide support							
Backup/Restore Mail	Provide memory		4 €					
	Backup Mail		7 €					
	Restore Mail		5 €					

Fig. 77. Function cost matrix (extract)

The cost analysis led to two exceptional insights. At the component level, the costs of servers and support made up the majority of costs (> 70%). At the function level the main functions "Manage User Accounts" and "Access Mobile" resulted in especially high costs.

On the basis of the actual state analysis and the subsequent evaluation, it was decided that two analyses would be focused on in the procedural follow-up:

- Server infrastructure
- Security functions

These two focal points were also in accord with given project goals.

Phase 2: Speculation Phase

During several moderated workshops, in which brainstorming methods were drawn on, possible solutions for server infrastructure and the security functions were developed (see Fig. 78).

Some solution types were rejected quickly because they were either not feasible or too expensive. The most promising potential solutions were discussed in a separate workshop in greater detail and analyzed, for example with respect to secondary functions.

Phase 3: Analysis Phase

Five solution proposals were selected for a further analysis. Initially the analysis focused on how the solution proposals would affect the level of function fulfillment and whether they could guarantee the reliability demanded by customers. A closer examination of cost efficiency and effectiveness was carried out for each solution proposal. Using cost estimations, the expected realization expenditures and prospective cost savings were forecasted and the effects on the unit cost per email account were calculated. An optimal saving potential of 36% was calculated with respect to server infrastructure. The more comprehensive security functions would result in a cost increase of 17%.

No.	Solution
Server-Infrastructure	
1	Total outsourcing
2	Use of blade servers
3	New system management tool
4	Change to Unix platform
5	ASP platform
6	Usage-based accounting
7	Virtualisation of ressources
8	Server consolidation
9	Scalable Platforms
10	...
Security functions	
20	SSL-based Web-access
21	Smartcard-Infrastructure
22	Trust-Center
23	Central Virus scanner
24	Spam service
25	...

Fig. 78. List of possible solutions (extract)

Phases 4 and 5: Planning and Presentation Phases

From the proposed solutions which were analyzed, four proposals were selected to plan in greater detail. In the context of the planning phase these proposals were specified in the form of technical and system concepts. Here value analysis does not greatly differ from well-known project processing procedures. The prepared solution proposals were presented to a decision-making body.

4.5 Potential and Limits of ITIL Within IIM[4]

In implementing service oriented information management processes, many IT service providers look to the Best Practices described in the IT Infrastructure Library (ITIL) (see Chapter 2.6). Opinions about the potential and limits of ITIL are highly inconsistent. ITIL has been praised in many publications as more or less a miracle weapon and universal remedy for IT service providers. However, con-

---

[4] The information presented in this chapter is based on the joint research of the authors and Axel Hochstein (see Hochstein et al. 2004b)

tradictory opinions also state that ITIL is only suitable for the organization of operational support and computing center processes and provides very little new information. Discussions about ITIL, often based on limited knowledge, lead to uncertainty and false expectations with regard to the chances and risks of an implementation of ITIL-based management processes. Can ITIL really represent a comprehensive management model for IT service providers, or is ITIL only applicable to a subareas of information management and, if so, which ones?

To follow up on this question, we examined how the contents of ITIL can be incorporated in the model of integrated information management. The potential and limits of ITIL can be demonstrated through this incorporation as in a GAP analysis. More precisely, this means posing the question: In what areas of information management does ITIL propose solutions and in what areas are no or only insufficient solutions proposed? Using the opposite reasoning these insights can be used in establishing the fine points of the IIM model. Within those areas, where ITIL has defined the Best Practice, ITIL descriptions can be used and do not have to be reinvented.

In this chapter the ITIL modules are presented in three layers of detail. Following this, the individual ITIL modules are incorporated in the IIM model and gaps are identified. The consequences for information management can then be derived from this GAP analysis.

4.5.1 The ITIL Modules and the Levels of Detail

An overview of the individual ITIL modules was already presented in Chapter 2.6. In examining ITIL contents it is easily seen that individual modules are described in various degrees of detail. For example, the modules Service Support and Service Delivery are described in greater detail than the modules Application Management or Business Perspective. Accordingly, ITIL contents can be categorized in the three levels of detail. For the modules with the greatest amount of detail, there are meticulous descriptions of the modules (approx. 25–80 pages for each), including goals, activities, some input/output schemes, cost–benefit perspectives, problems and challenges, key operational figures, role schemes, documents, and methods. In Fig. 79 modules with the greatest degree of detail are illustrated in white. The modules in the second layer of detail are characterized by less detailed descriptions (approx. 15–50 pages) and an incomplete explanation of goals, activities, input/output schemes, cost–benefit perspectives, problems and challenges, role schemes, documents, and methods. These modules are shaded gray in Fig.791. Finally, the modules with the lowest degree of detail are characterized by short descriptions (approx. 3–7 pages), whereby goals, activities, input/output schemes, etc. are completely missing. These modules are shown in black in Fig. 79.

4.5.2 Incorporation of ITIL in the IIM Model

Next, the individual ITIL module tasks are assigned to the components of the IIM model to determine where the potential and limits of ITIL lie. The assignment of the tasks of the ITIL module "Business Perspective" is missing here because this book has not yet been published.

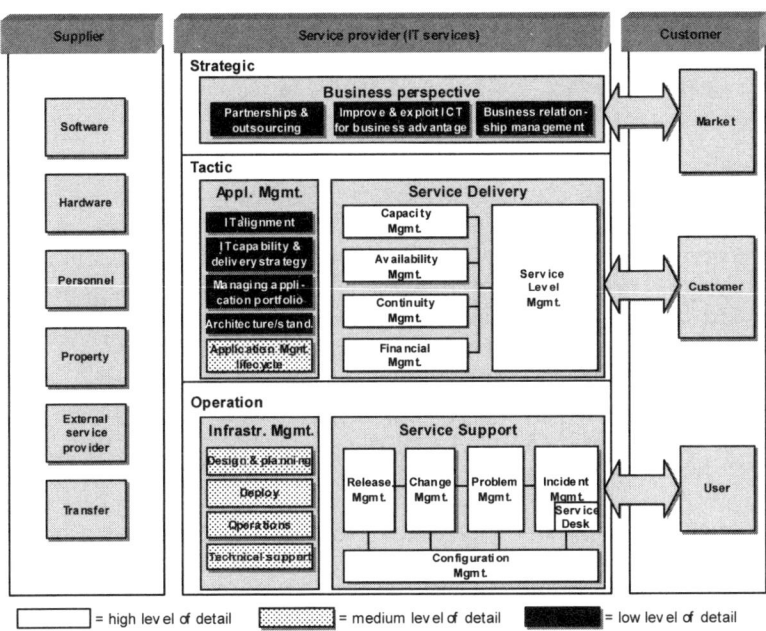

Fig. 79. Levels of detail in the ITIL

ITIL Modules with a High Level of Detail

The modules with the highest degree of detail are Service Delivery and Service Support. Service Delivery is divided into the processes Service Level Management, Capacity Management, Availability Management, Continuity Management, and Financial Management. Service Support is divided into the processes Incident Management, Problem Management, Change Management, Release Management, and Configuration Management.

Some of the tasks of ITIL Service Delivery are described in the IIM model as the interface between the service provider's Delivery Planning and the customer's Sourcing Planning. For example, within the context of *Service Level Management* the tasks concerning the creation of an SLA, the regular evaluation of the agreed

SLA, and Expectation Management, which should guarantee a realistic customer expectation of the provided IT products, are described. The monitoring of the agreed product efficiency and effectiveness and the production of SLA reports are operational activities of Customer Management and have thus been assigned to Delivery Controlling in the IIM model. If the agreed SLA should be threatened, then improvement measures must be initiated. The IIM model includes several units in the concrete planning of these measures. Thereby, Production Planning and Controlling, as well as Delivery Planning and Controlling are responsible for elaborating on suggestions as to how to optimize the product. Serious problems must be addressed at the planning level, and smaller problems can be solved operationally at the controlling level. Continuous supervision and maintenance of internal and external service contracts is assigned to the modules Delivery and Production Controlling in the IIM model.

The *Capacity Management* in ITIL is divided into the three categories: Business, Service, and Resource Capacity Management. The task of Business Capacity Management is to identify future business requirements of IT products on time, and to plan and implement the necessary measures proactively. In the IIM model Business Capacity Management is assigned to Delivery Planning because the customer is directly involved. In ITIL Service Capacity Management entails the capacity-related monitoring of the agreed service levels, so that this task is assigned to Delivery Controlling. Here there is a close link to Resource Capacity Management, within which the operational rates of utilization of production infrastructure (e.g. server, networks, etc.) are monitored and evaluated. Thus, in the IIM model, Resource Capacity Management can be found within Production Controlling. ITIL also addresses the additional provision of capacity- relevant data and the creation of significant capacity plans. Providing capacity-relevant data is a task of Production Controlling. Capacity plans are taken into account in Production Planning. Under the concept of Demand Management, ITIL combines activities which can affect users' demands for IT products in such a way that short-term capacity bottlenecks can be avoided. In the IIM model this is a common task of Delivery and Production Controlling. Application Dimensioning and Modeling are additional tasks and methods of ITIL Capacity Management. These are taken into account in Development Planning.

Availability Management guarantees that the provided IT products match business requirements and that the IT service provider can guarantee a cost effective and sustainable level of availability. Initially, Development, Production, and Delivery Planning must collectively plan a customer specific availability of the individual IT products. The availability requirements are assessed in Delivery Planning. Subsequently, Development and Production Planning must guarantee that the requirements can be met by the applications and infrastructures. The initiation and implementation of measures for subsequently improving availability is a responsibility of Delivery Controlling, and both Development and Production Controlling are also involved. All of the monitoring of product availability and/or the measurement of the availability of individual resources takes place in the context of Production and Delivery Controlling.

IT Service Continuity Management must ensure that if a system crash occurs, IT products are restored within a period previously agreed upon with the customer and that go around measures are available. A Continuity Strategy is defined in cooperation with the business units. In the IIM model this is assigned to Production Planning. The planning and implementation of Recovery Measures are essentially tasks belonging to Production Planning, whereby interfaces exist, when necessary, to Development Planning, Development Controlling, and Production Controlling. Production controlling is responsible for the operational management of Recovery Mechanisms and the management of potential ensuing demands.

Within ITIL *Financial Management* covers the topics of budgeting, controlling, and accounting. Within the context of budgeting, financial resources are allocated to the individual IT projects and/or products. Within the IIM model this task belongs to Portfolio Planning. Controlling enables costs to be correctly assigned to IT products, so that cost–benefit analyses can be made. The cost assessment takes place within Production and Development Controlling. The Controlling process for IT products is a task of Portfolio Controlling. Delivery Controlling prepares customer oriented reports and key figures. Product accounting and invoicing is a task belonging to Delivery Controlling.

Incident Management is responsible for tasks concerning the acceptance and management of error reports and customer inquiries. It is also in charge of the coordination, monitoring, and communication of how customers' inquiries or error reports are being handled. Thus Incident Management represents the operational interface to users and is assigned to Production Controlling. The Service Desk, which manages the Incident Management process, is a part of production.

In Incident Management errors and faults are received and handled. However, the goal of *Problem Management* is to quickly and proactively identify and repair the problems causing the errors. Within the IIM model the problem and error reactive tasks as well as proactive problem management are assigned to Production Controlling. Furthermore, Production Controlling is responsible for the preparation and provision of problem-relevant information.

Change Management guarantees that IT relevant changes, at tactical or operational levels, transpire within a general framework of standardized Change Management procedures and under consistent Change Management regulations. Depending upon the nature of the change, various IT service creation units may be called in on the Change Management Process. Not only Delivery, Production, and Development Planning but also Portfolio Planning may be called in when changes are far-reaching and important. This will be the case, for example, if the changes have direct effects on certain IT products and, especially, if authorization is needed. Then again acceptance, handling, and coordination of application system and infrastructure specific changes are assigned to Development and Production Planning and/or, when the changes are small enough, to Development and Production Controlling.

Release Management is responsible for planning, developing, and implementing software and hardware releases, such that requirements are met. The planning of new releases is a task of Development and Production Planning. The development and implementation of releases takes place operationally in the context of Development and Production Controlling.

Configuration Management is responsible for regulating and coordinating IT infrastructure and IT products (see Ex. 5, Chapter 2.5). A logical model of the infrastructure and products is created, in which the so-called Configuration Items (CIs) are identified, checked, maintained, and verified. Examples of typical CIs are servers, network components, desktops, or software licenses; also, disruptions, service inquiries, identified errors, SLAs, internal service contracts, service contracts with suppliers, information about suppliers, employees, physical locations, or business units. The tasks of Configuration Management are assigned to Production Controlling because it essentially deals with the administration and provision of configuration-relevant information.

ITIL Modules with a Medium Level of Detail

The strengths of ITIL lie without a doubt in the modules Service Delivery and Service Support. The modules ICT Infrastructure Management and Application Management have clearly less detailed information.

The module *Application Management* covers the crucial tasks necessary for managing the application system life cycle. Thereby, ITIL follows the classical procedural models of software development and differentiates between the phases Requirements, Design, Build, Deploy, Operate, and Optimize. Within the IIM model the requirement analysis takes place in Delivery Planning. The other phases of ITIL Application Management are tasks belonging to Development Planning and Controlling.

ICT Infrastructure Management describes the phases and tasks of the IT infrastructure life cycle. The Design and Planning Phases are first and foremost concerned with providing development and implementation guidelines for an IT infrastructure, which fulfills requirements. Correspondingly, ITIL covers the areas of technology (e.g. mainframes, distributed systems, networks, desktops, and mobile devices), architectures, operational processes, and management methods. These tasks belong to Production Strategy and Production Planning. In the Deployment Phase, the ICT Infrastructure is implemented according to the requirements defined in the Design and Planning Phases. Production Planning is responsible for this task. The ITIL Operation Process guarantees an effective, operational management of IT infrastructure, including the necessary organization and maintenance. It thus represents the core task of operational Production Controlling. Technical Support is presented in the form of a "technical center of excellence," in which competent technical know-how from Operation and Deployment is made available. Production Planning is responsible for Technical Support.

ITIL Modules with a Low Level of Detail

ITIL modules with the lowest level of detail are made up of only very general descriptions. Thus, here too, a detailed description has been forgone.

Fig. 80 presents an overview of the assignment of ITIL modules to the IIM model. It is apparent that ITIL covers only some subtopics. ITIL provides merely a few very general references as to Supplier and Portfolio Management as well as to the strategic areas of Development, Production, and Customer Management. However, ITIL contents are very applicable and appropriate for the planning and controlling topics in Development, Production, and Customer Management. But also here, ITIL does not cover all of the required tasks. In ITIL important model elements such as tasks, role allocations, documents, methods, or input/outputs are dealt with incompletely or not at all. For example, in ITIL there is no reference to the tasks necessary for employing customer- and segment-specific communication instruments (e.g. advertising measures) or steering distribution of IT products, which are more or less made up of hardware.

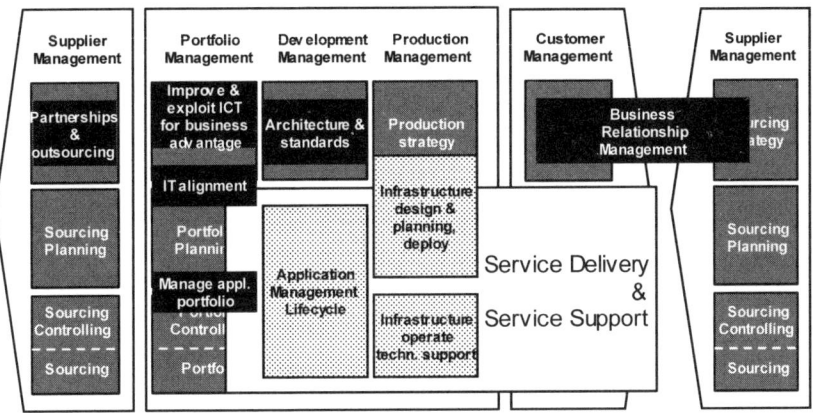

Fig. 80. Assignment of ITIL modules to the IIM model

For information management this means that for the design and organization of service oriented IT product manufacturing, ITIL is insufficient. It is an unrealistic expectation that only by introducing ITIL-compliant management processes, IT service providers can gain a competitive advantage. There are additional management tasks and topics to be considered other than those in ITIL. The preceding analysis and a closer look at the IIM model provide references. Nevertheless, implementing ITIL can be beneficial when the influence of existing and established Best Practices flows into the operational management of development, production, and customer processes.

5 Summary and Future Prospects

As in a Management Summary, in conclusion we would like to recapitulate the main results and insights, as well as present some prospects for future topics and emphasis, which are necessary for a better understanding and incorporation of the presented model.

In our work we were led by two principles. The first principle is that all processes and tasks in information management are consistently product oriented. The second principle is that successful management concepts from industrial manufacturing must be integrated into IT service production.

The essence of a product oriented perspective is the output of IT service production (i.e. IT products and IT services). From a customer and user perspective, an IT product is a bundle of IT services, which supports a business process or a business product. In light of a consistent customer orientation in IT service production, all information management activities must be aligned to the goal of producing customer-required products efficiently and effectively. The product oriented approach has many advantages, such as:

- It increases the effectiveness of IT units by implementing customer oriented management methods.
- It improves collaboration with customers and thus facilitates an optimal consideration of customer requirements in designing products.
- It increases the transparency of products by organizing and designing product catalogs.
- It is more efficient because there is a consistent cost accounting and calculation.
- It promotes the marketability of IT units by the implementation of pricing procedures.

Even though the use of product oriented management concepts is not yet of common practice in information management, for many years their application has played a central role in other industries. Information management can profit from this wealth of experience, applying successful management concepts from other industries (e.g. manufacturing or service) by assuming or adapting these concepts. This applies especially to the concepts of cost and product accounting, quality management, production planning and controlling, product program planning, and integrated product production.

The model of integrated information management introduced here presents a framework, which can be used for converting to a product oriented information management. The processes Source, Make, and Deliver encompass the procurement, production, and sales tasks of an IT service provider:

- One responsibility of an IT service provider's *Source Process* is to procure the IT product's externally manufactured product components. The customer's Source Process is responsible for purchasing the IT service provider's IT products.

- The *Make Process* encompasses all tasks necessary for the production of IT products.

- The *Deliver Process* is the IT service provider's customer interface and includes all sales, distribution, and marketing tasks for IT products.

Implementing integrated information management concepts, using the Source, Make, Deliver principle, has a number of significant consequences:

- Introducing *Product Portfolio Management* to both IT service providers and their customers: The customer's product portfolio depicts customer IT product requirements. It thus represents demand. The IT service provider's product portfolio includes its current IT products. Thus it represents supply. The product portfolio must be presented as a product catalog, in which IT product functionality, quality, and costs are described from a customer viewpoint.

- Introduction of *life cycle oriented management concepts*: In the context of Portfolio Management, IT products must be life cycle oriented, i.e. they must be actively designed, organized, and controlled with respect to time. Life cycle orientation takes into consideration both a sales oriented perspective (development phase, introduction phase ... downturn phase) and a manufacturing oriented perspective (planning, initial development ... retirement).

- Introduction of *cost accounting for IT products* including product result accounting: Cost objects (IT products), cost centers (IT services), and cost categories (IT resources) are united in an efficient actual and target cost accounting. This enables the calculation of IT product unit costs, as well as the allocation of costs of IT resources actually used to the individual sold IT products.

- Introduction of *Consistent Quality Management*: Quality Management is not based on production oriented figures, i.e. technical, quality characteristics, for example, availability, response time, or turnover. Instead the definition of customer-specific, guaranteed quality characteristics of IT products is emphasized, for example the advantages and cost savings in business processes or customer satisfaction. Additional tasks are monitoring current levels of quality and reporting. The costs of non-quality ("cost of poor quality") are of special importance to both the customer and IT service provider.

- Introduction of *standard processes*: Existing reference process models, e.g. ITIL or COBIT, are used in implementing standardized management processes.

- Management focus is on the *production of IT products*: Management will no longer concentrate on many isolated IT projects, but instead the planning, development, and production of IT products will be jointly designed, organized, and steered.

The concepts and solution proposals presented in this book are only a first step toward a product oriented information management. The model introduced here should be thought of as a general framework. It enables a positioning and combined allocation of individual topic areas and tasks. In many individual areas, the content must be more precisely described, methods supplemented, and practically tested applications added.

At the "Integrated Information Management" Competence Center, as a part of the University of St. Gallen Institute for Information Management, we work together with several commercial partners on these conceptual ideas and further exploratory questions. Based on the ideas presented in this book in the coming years, concrete procedural models and solutions for practical use will continually evolve.

6 References

Balzert H. (1998): Lehrbuch der Software-Technik: Software-Management, Software-Qualitätssicherung, Unternehmensmodellierung. Vol. 2. Spektrum, Berlin.

Balzert H. (2000): Lehrbuch der Software-Technik: Software-Entwicklung. Vol. 1, 2nd ed. Spektrum, Berlin.

Boeh A., Meyer M. (2004): IT-Balanced Scorecard: Ein Ansatz zur strategischen Ausrichtung der IT. In: Zarnekow R., Brenner W., Grohmann H. H. (eds.): Informationsmanagement – Konzepte und Strategien für die Praxis, dpunkt, Heidelberg.

Brunner H., Gasser K., Pörtig F. (2004): Strategische Informatikplanung – Ein Erfahrungsbericht. HMD – Praxis der Wirtschaftsinformatik, Nr. 232.

Cap Gemini Ernst & Young (2003): Studie IT-Trends 2003: Wohin geht die Reise? Berlin.

Carr N. G. (2003): IT Doesn't Matter. Harvard Business Review, May, pp. 41–49.

Deutsche Telekom (2001): Produktkatalog ZB Billing Services. Darmstadt.

Dietrich L., Schirra W. (2004): IT im Unternehmen – Leistungssteigerung bei sinkenden Budgets – Erfolgsbeispiele aus der Praxis. Springer, Berlin.

Dumke R., Rautenstrauch C., Schmietendorf A., Scholz A. (2001): Performance Engineering: State of the Art and Current Trends. Springer, Berlin.

Ellermann H. (2003): IT bei den DAX-30-Unternehmen. CIO, Vol. 3, Januar/Februar, pp. 12–18.

Eversheim W. (1990): Organisation in der Produktionstechnik. Vol. 1, 2nd ed. VDI-Verlag, Düsseldorf.

Fürer P. (1994): Prozesse und EDV-Kostenrechnung – Die prozessbasierte Verrechnungskonzeption für Bankrechenzentren. Bern.

Heinen E. (1991): Industriebetriebslehre: Entscheidungen im Industriebetrieb. 9th ed. Gabler, Wiesbaden.

Hinterhuber H. H. (1992): Strategische Unternehmensführung, Vol 1. Strategisches Denken, Berlin.

Hochstein A., Zarnekow R., Brenner W. (2004a): Service-orientiertes IT-Management nach ITIL – Möglichkeiten und Grenzen. HMD – Praxis der Wirtschaftsinformatik, Vol. 41, No. 239, pp. 68–76.

Hochstein A., Wetzel Y., Brenner W. (2004b): Case study: ITIL-konformer Service Desk bei T-Mobile Deutschland. HMD – Praxis der Wirtschaftsinformatik, Vol. 41, No. 237, pp.32–42.

Hoffmann H. J. (1994): Wertanalyse – Die westliche Antwort auf Kaizen. Ullstein, Frankfurt am Main.

ISACA (2004): Cobit, 3rd ed. www.isaca.org/cobit.htm.

References

IT Governance Institute (2003): Board Briefing on IT Governance, 2nd ed. Rolling Meadows, www.itgovernance.org.

Jahn H. C., Meyer T. D., al-Ani A., Ackermann W., Bechmann T., El Hage B. (2002): Informationstechnologie als Wettbewerbsfaktor. Studie Accenture und Universität St. Gallen.

Jouanne-Diedrich H. v. (2004): 15 Jahre Outsourcing-Forschung: Systematisierung und Lessons Learned. In: Zarnekow R., Brenner W., Grohmann H. H. (eds.): Informationsmanagement – Konzepte und Strategien für die Praxis, dpunkt, Heidelberg, pp. 125–133.

Kotler P. (2002): Marketing Management. Prentice Hall, London.

Lamberti H.-J. (2002): Herausforderungen an die IT in einem globalen Finanzdienstleister. Guest lecture at the University of St. Gallen, 5 November 2002.

Mai J. (1996): Konzeption einer controllinggerechten Kosten- und Leistungsrechnung für Rechenzentren. Frankfurt am Main.

Matys E. (2002): Praxishandbuch Produktmanagement. Campus, Frankfurt.

Miles L. (1972): Techniques of Value Analysis and Engineering. 2nd ed. New York.

OGC (2000): ITIL – Best Practice for Service Support. The Stationary Office, Norwich.

OGC (2002): ITIL – Best Practice for ICT Infrastructure Management. The Stationary Office, Norwich.

Schmutte A. M. (2002): Six Sigma im Business Excellence Prozess. In: Bühner R. (ed.): Organisation, loose-leaf edition. Verlag Moderne Industrie, Munich.

Schweitzer M. (1994): Industriebetriebslehre. 2nd ed. Franz Vahlen, Munich.

Sebastian K.-H., Maessen A. (2003): Strategisches Preismanagement. In: Campus Management. Vol. 1. Campus Verlag, Frankfurt/Main, pp. 418–421.

Stone L. (2002a): Matching enterprise needs with the right external sources. Gartner Research Note, No. K-18-3939.

Stone L. (2002b): Critical Success Factors for Outsourcing Relationships. Gartner Research Article Top View, No. AV-18-1098.

Supply Chain Council (2003): Supply-Chain Operations Reference Model: Overview Version 6.0. Supply-Chain Council Inc., Pittsburgh.

Thiel W. (2002): IT-Strategien zur aktuellen Marktlage. 8th Handelsblatt Congress Strategic IT Management, Bonn, 29 January 2002.

Zarnekow R., Scheeg J., Brenner W. (2004): Untersuchung der Lebenszykluskosten von IT-Anwendungen. Wirtschaftsinformatik, Vol. 46, No. 3, pp. 81–87.

Zarnekow R., Hochstein A., Brenner W. (2005): Serviceorientiertes IT-Management – ITIL Best Practices und Fallstudien. Springer, Berlin.

Zeithaml V. A., Berry L. L., Parasuraman A. (1988): Communication and control processes in the delivery of service quality. Journal of Marketing, Vol. 52, No. 2, pp. 35–48.

Zentrum Wertanalyse (1995): Wertanalyse: Idee – Methode – System. 5th ed. VDI-Verlag, Düsseldorf.

Zrimsek B., Eisenfeld B., Nelson S. (2003): Defining the Business Application Life Cycle. Gartner Research Report, 04.09.2003, No. TU-20-8836.

7 About the Authors

Dr. Ruediger Zarnekow (ruediger.zarnekow@unisg.ch) is Project Manager at the Institute for Information Management at the University of St. Gallen. Since 2002 he has held the position of Head of the "Integrated Information Management" Competence Center He is particularly involved in trends and developments in information management and electronic procurement. Dr. Zarnekow made his doctorate at the University of Freiberg with "The Possible Application of Software Agents in Electronic Commerce". He was employed from 1995 to 1998 at T-Systems Multimedia Solutions GmbH, as Head of Electronic Commerce. He studied information management at the European Business School, Oestrich-Winkel, and also received a Master of Science in Advanced Software Technologies from the University of Wolverhampton, England.

Professor Walter Brenner (walter.brenner@unisg.ch) is Professor of Information Management at the University of St. Gallen and Acting Director of the Institute for Information Management. From 1999 to 2001 he was Professor of Information Management and Business Administration at the University of Essen. From 1993 to 1999 he was Professor for General Business Administration and Information Management at the University of Freiberg. From 1989 to 1993 he led the research program Information Management 2000 at the Institute for Information Management at the University of St. Gallen. Professor Brenner worked at Alusuisse Lonza AG in Basel from 1985 to 1989, finally as Director of Application Development. He studied and made his doctorate from 1978 to 1985 at the University of St. Gallen. The focus of his research is within information management, Customer Relationship Management, and new technologies. He is an active freelancing advisor in questions pertaining to information management and company preparations for the digital networked world. Professor Brenner has published 13 books and more than 120 articles. He is a member of many advisory and supervisory boards and boards of directors.

Uwe Pilgram (uwe.pilgram@t-system.com) studied economics in Tübingen. From 1967 to 1984 he worked at IBM Germany in managerial positions in Application Development, Product Management, and Sales. Afterwards he assisted in founding the data processing subsidiary of the Metallgesellschaft MGI, one of the first IT subsidiaries of a company in Germany. Later, he led BASF group-wide Application Development and a project to consolidate the BASF European computing centers. Subsequently, he was named Head of the Consolidated Computer Centers. Since 1995 Mr. Pilgram has worked at Deutsche Telekom. There he has led the IT operation of T-Mobil Germany and designed the Group's strategic IT management. Currently he is involved in the development of the Group's external IT business. Mr. Pilgram is married and has two daughters.